TIME LIFE BOOKS

52 Easy Weekend HOME IMPROVEMENTS

A Year's Worth of Money-Saving Projects

TIME® LIFE BOOKS

Time-Life Books is a division of Time Life Inc.

TIME LIFE INC.

PRESIDENT & CEO: George Artandi

TIME-LIFE TRADE PUBLISHING

VICE PRESIDENT AND PUBLISHER:	Neil Levin
Senior Director of Acquisitions and Editorial Resources:	Jennifer Pearce
Director of New Product Development:	Carolyn Clark
Director of Trade Sales:	Dana Coleman
Director of Marketing:	Inger Forland
Director of New Product Development:	Teresa Graham
Director of Custom Publishing:	John Lalor
Director of Special Markets:	Robert Lombardi
Director of Creative Services:	Laura McNeill
Technical Specialist:	Monika Lynde
Project Manager:	Jennifer L. Ward
Production Manager:	Carolyn Bounds
Director of Quality Assurance:	James D. King

Adapted from HOME REPAIR MADE EASY binder card set.

Editor:	Lee Hassig
Deputy Editor:	Kathleen Mallow
Marketing Director:	James Gillespie
Associate Editor/Research & Writing:	Karen Sweet

HOME REPAIR MADE EASY was produced for Time Life Inc. by ST. REMY MULTIMEDIA INC.
Adaptation was produced by ALLEN D. BRAGDON PUBLISHERS, INC.

TIME-LIFE is a trademark of Time Warner Inc., and affiliated companies.
Printed in China
10 9 8 7 6 5 4 3 2 1

Library of Congress Cataloging-in-Publication Data
52 Easy Weekend Home Improvements: A Year's Worth of Money-Saving Projects
  p. cm.
    ISBN: 0-7370-0009-0 (hardcover)
    ISBN: 0-7835-5307-2 (softcover)
    ISBN: 0-7370-0314-6 (spiral binding)
  1. Dwellings—Maintenance and repair—Amateur's manuals. I. Time-Life Books.
TH4817.3.A12   1998   97-42910
643'.7—dc21   CIP

Cover design:	Studio A
Picture Credits:	Cover photograph: © TSM/Jean Miele, 1998
	Studio Photographer: Robert Chartier
	Adaptation Photographs: Frank Fosters; pages 18-21/32-33/46-47/58-63/82-85/86-87/112-115/118-119/128-129/140-141/146-149/188-191.

Books produced by Time-Life Custom Publishing are available at a special bulk discount for promotional and premium use. Custom adaptations can also be created to meet your specific marketing goals. Call 1-800-323-5255.

TIME LIFE BOOKS

52 Easy Weekend HOME IMPROVEMENTS

A Year's Worth of Money-Saving Projects

By the Editors of Time-Life Books, Alexandria, Virginia

CONTENTS

HOME SYSTEMS	**PAGE 6**
1. Unclogging a Bathtub Drain	8
2. Replacing a Toilet Ballcock	10
3. Repairing a Copper Pipe	12
4. Adding a Bathroom Vanity	16
5. Fixing Faucet Leaks & Drips	18
6. Installing a Double-handle Faucet Set	22
7. Servicing a Water Heater	24
8. Mounting Smoke Detectors	30
9. Installing a CO Detector	32
10. Mounting a Ceiling Fan	34
11. Installing a Dimmer Switch	36
12. Installing a GFCI Outlet	38
13. Replacing a Lamp Socket	40
14. Insulating an Attic	42
15. Weatherproofing a Door	44
16. Installing a Motion Detector	46

INTERIOR REPAIRS AND IMPROVEMENTS	**PAGE 48**
17. Preparing Surfaces for Paint or Wallpaper	50
18. Painting Interior Walls & Ceilings	54
19. Wallpapering a Room	58
20. Hanging a Wallcovering Border	64
21. Repairing Wallcoverings	68
22. Regrouting Rigid Tiles	72
23. Replacing a Laminate Countertop	74
24. Refacing Cabinets	78
25. Installing Molding & Chair Rails	82
26. Hanging Frames on Different Walls	86
27. Correcting Interior Doors	88
28. Framing an Interior Wall	94
29. Hanging Drywall	98
30. Repairing Drywall Holes	104
31. Repairing Interior Foundation Cracks	106

EXTERIOR REPAIRS AND IMPROVEMENTS	**PAGE 110**
32. Painting Exterior Window Trim	112
33. Maintaining Gutters & Downspouts	116
34. Repairing Gutters & Downspouts	118
35. Replacing Asphalt Shingles	122

36. Waterproofing Brick & Cement 128
37. Replacing Window Screens 130
38. Installing a Prehung Window 132
39. Replacing a Window Pane 136
40. Adding Locks to Windows 140
41. Adding a Deadbolt Lockset 142

OUTDOOR STRUCTURES AND LANDSCAPING **PAGE 144**

42. Staining Outdoor Structures 146
43. Framing a Ground-level Deck 150
44. Laying Deck Flooring 156
45. Putting Up a Deck Railing 160
46. Repairing Deck Posts 162
47. Building a Board-on-board Fence 164
48. Enclosing a Porch with Screens 168
49. Laying Sand-bed Brick Paving 172
50. Building a Deck Bench 178
51. Starting a Lawn 182
52. Controlling Ground Water Runoff 188

TOOLS AND TECHNIQUES **PAGE 192**

The Home Workshop 194
Personal Safety Gear 196
Measurers & Markers 198
Using Straightedges, Squares, & T-bevels 199
Hammers 203
Fastening with Screws 204
Cutters 208
Handsaws 209
Wrenches 210
Pliers and Clamps 211
Planes & Files 212
Chisels, Awls & Punches 213
Power Tools 214
Plumber's Aids 216
General Tools 217
Dealing with Hazards 219
Dealing with Emergencies 221

APPENDIX: CALENDAR OF HOME MAINTENANCE **PAGE 222**

IMPORTANT TELEPHONE NUMBERS **PAGE 223**

HOME
SYSTEMS

PROJECT		PAGE
1	Unclogging a Bathtub Drain	8
2	Replacing a Toilet Ballcock	10
3	Repairing a Copper Pipe	12
4	Adding a Bathroom Vanity	16
5	Fixing Faucet Leaks & Drips	18
6	Installing a Double-handle Faucet Set	22
7	Servicing a Water Heater	24
8	Mounting Smoke Detectors	30
9	Installing a CO Detector	32
10	Mounting a Ceiling Fan	34
11	Installing a Dimmer Switch	36
12	Installing a GFCI Outlet	38
13	Replacing a Lamp Socket	40
14	Insulating an Attic	42
15	Weatherproofing a Door	44
16	Installing a Motion Detector	46

1 Unclogging a Bathtub Drain

$ Estimated Savings: $60

BEFORE YOU START
◆ Check if other drains are blocked or slow; if so, the problem may originate elsewhere in the plumbing system.
◆ To prepare a bathtub for clearing out a clog, remove the drain fittings.

Disconnecting Drain Fittings

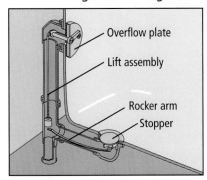

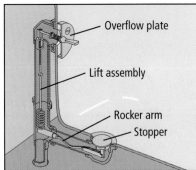

For pop-up drains *(above)*, pull up the stopper and work out the rocker arm, then unscrew the overflow plate and slide out the lift assembly.

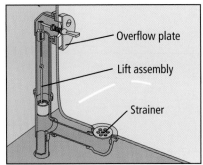

On a trip-lever drain *(above)*, there is no stopper; remove only the overflow plate and lift assembly.

WHAT YOU NEED

Tools
✔ Force-cup plunger
✔ Trap-and-drain auger
✔ Garden hose
✔ Threaded adapter
✔ Expansion nozzle

Materials
✔ Rags

SAFETY FIRST

To avoid the risk of contact with a chemical drain cleaner, apply it only after clearing the main clog. Remove a garden hose from the drain immediately after flushing a clog to prevent waste water from entering the supply system.

Plunging. Plug the overflow opening with a wet rag. Add enough water to cover the cup of a plunger, then pump it vigorously up and down over the drain *(above)*. (To improve the cup's seal, coat the rim with petroleum jelly.)

Augering. Feed a trap-and-drain auger into the overflow opening *(above)* and crank the handle clockwise to break up the clog. Keep cranking the handle clockwise while backing out the auger to avoid losing debris causing the blockage.

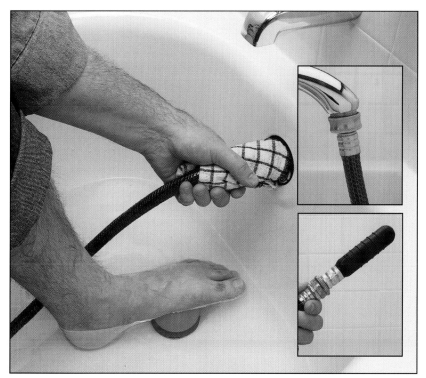

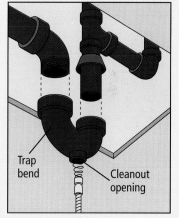

Flushing. Connect a garden hose to an indoor faucet with a threaded adapter *(upper inset)*. Feed the hose into the overflow opening and seal around it with a wet rag, then plug the drain *(above)* while having the water turned on full force and off. Alternatively, fit the hose with an expansion nozzle *(lower inset)*.
CAUTION: Disconnect the hose and let the nozzle deflate before removing it.

CLEARING THE TRAP BEND

Trap bend

Cleanout opening

When all else fails, access to the trap bend is required to unclog the drain—which usually means cutting an opening in the ceiling directly below it. Unscrew the cleanout plug to feed in a trap-and-drain auger *(above)*; if there is no plug, take off the trap bend. Auger into the drainpipe first toward the tub, then toward the main drain.

2 Replacing a Toilet Ballcock
💲 Estimated Savings: $60

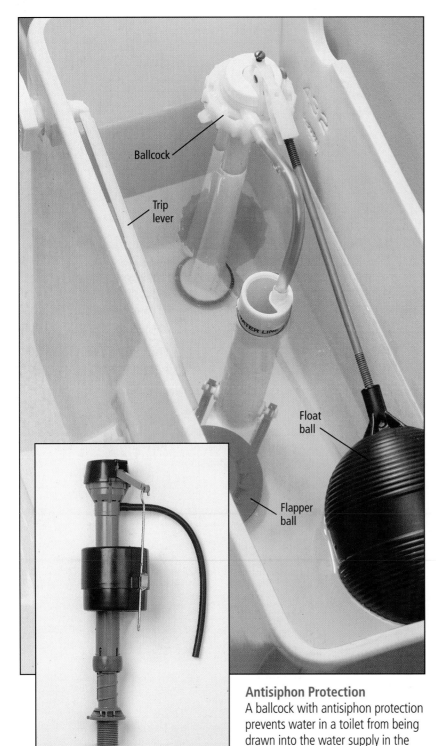

Ballcock

Trip lever

Float ball

Flapper ball

BEFORE YOU START

Signs of a faulty toilet ballcock include water running constantly, vibration as the tank fills and a high-pitched whine during flushing, but check first for other possible causes:

◆ If the flapper ball isn't seated properly, reposition the lift chain or wire on the handle's trip lever.

◆ If the float ball is cracked and full of water, unscrew it from the float arm and install a replacement.

Adjusting the Float Ball

Gently bend the float arm to stop the float ball from rubbing and to change the water level: down to raise it; up to lower it *(above)*.

Antisiphon Protection

A ballcock with antisiphon protection prevents water in a toilet from being drawn into the water supply in the event of a drop in water pressure—and may be required by local codes.

WHAT YOU NEED

Tools
✔ Adjustable wrench
✔ Locking pliers

Materials
✔ Replacement ballcock
✔ Sponge

SAFETY FIRST

Turn off the water supply to the toilet and hold down the handle to drain as much water as possible from the tank.

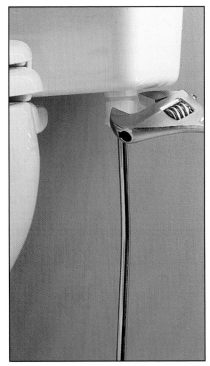

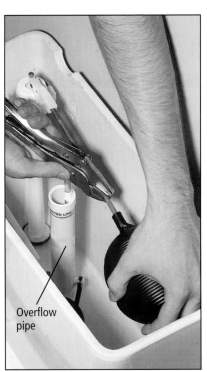

Overflow
pipe

1 **Sponge up water** left in the tank, then unscrew the coupling nut and remove the supply tube; if necessary, use an adjustable wrench *(above)*.

2 **Unscrew the float arm** and ball from the ballcock, using locking pliers to grip and turn the arm *(above)*. Take the refill tube off the overflow pipe.

3 **With locking pliers** clamped to the ballcock and wedged in the tank *(above, top)*, loosen the locknut under the tank *(above, bottom)* and unscrew it, then remove the ballcock.

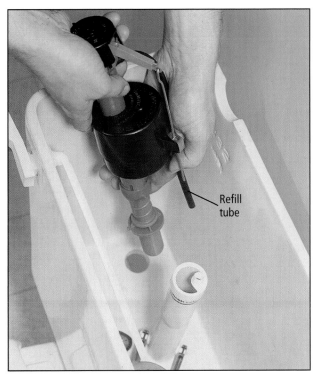

Refill
tube

4 **Adjust a new ballcock** to the height of the tank *(above)* and secure it with a locknut. Put the refill tube into the overflow pipe, then reconnect the supply tube.

5 **Turn on the water** and flush the toilet. Pinch and slide the clip on the float cup to adjust the water level: up to raise it; down to lower it *(above)*.

11

3 Repairing a Copper Pipe
[$] Estimated Savings: $80

BEFORE YOU START

◆ Replacement pipe and couplings must be of the same inside diameter—called nominal size—as the existing pipe. To determine a copper pipe's inside diameter without cutting it, measure its outside diameter and then subtract $\frac{1}{8}$ inch.

◆ Check if local building codes permit substituting CPVC pipe for copper pipe. PVC or other plastic may be allowed for cold-water supply pipes, but each type requires the use of its own particular primer and cement.

◆ Temporarily plug a pinhole leak by jamming in and breaking off the tip of a pencil or toothpick, then wrap the pipe with overlapping layers of electrical tape. Alternatively, use an old inner tube and secure it with hose clamps or install a pipe-leak clamp.

PIPE-LEAK CLAMP

Disassemble the clamp and fit the two halves around the damaged pipe so that the rubber gasket seals the leak. Insert and tighten the screws (*above*).

SAFETY FIRST

Turn off the water at the main shutoff, then open faucets and flush toilets to drain the supply pipes. Wear safety goggles and work gloves when soldering.

WHAT YOU NEED

Tools
✔ Tube cutter or hacksaw
✔ File
✔ Wire fitting brush
✔ Flux brush
✔ Propane torch
Materials
✔ Replacement copper pipe
✔ Couplings
✔ Plumber's abrasive sandcloth
✔ Paste flux

✔ Flameproof pad
✔ Solder

SUBSTITUTING CPVC PIPE
Tools
✔ Tube cutter or hacksaw and file
✔ Backsaw and miter box
✔ Paring knife
Materials
✔ Replacement CPVC pipe
✔ Compression-type couplings
✔ CPVC primer and cement

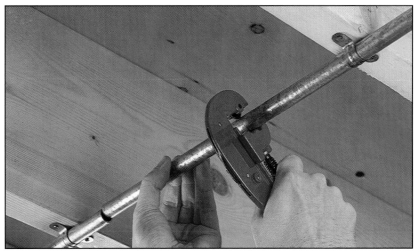

1 **Remove the length** of pipe to be replaced with a tube cutter *(above)*, tightening the cutting wheel after each rotation until it severs the pipe. (If the ends are difficult to reach, use a hacksaw.)

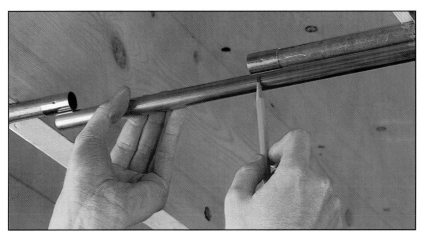

2 **Fit couplings** temporarily onto the ends of the standing pipe and mark the replacement pipe to length *(above)*. Cut the pipe to size with the tube cutter.

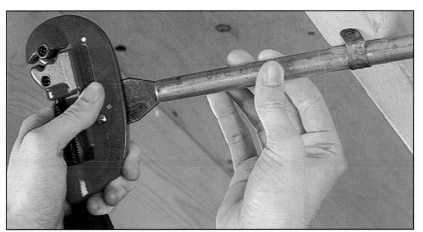

3 **Ream the ends** of the replacement and standing pipes *(above)*, then file off the ridge where the couplings will fit. (Remove the inner burr left by a hacksaw using a round file.)

BENDING OPTIONS

Slip a coiled-spring pipe bender onto the pipe. Clamp the bender in a vise and bend the pipe by hand *(above)*.

Fit the pipe into the slot of an electrical conduit bender. Push down on the bender handle to bend the pipe *(above)*.

13

4 Clean outside surfaces of the pipes that will contact couplings by rubbing with plumber's abrasive sandcloth *(far left)*. Scour the inside contact surfaces of the couplings using a wire fitting brush *(near left)*. **Caution:** Don't touch the cleaned surfaces; even small amounts of skin oil can weaken solder joints.

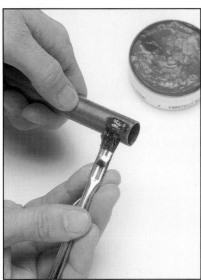

5 Brush a light coat of flux over the cleaned surfaces of the couplings and pipes *(far left)*. Slide the couplings onto the ends of the standing pipes *(near left)*, then push them far enough apart to insert the replacement pipe. Twist each coupling a quarter-turn to spread the flux evenly.

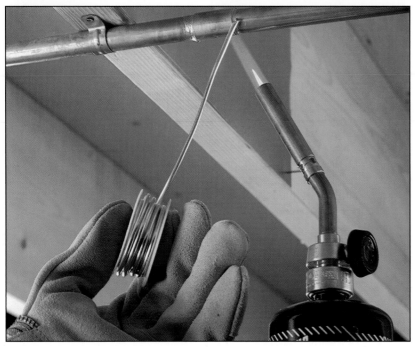

6 Mount a flameproof pad behind the repair and use a propane torch to solder each joint. Play the tip of the torch flame evenly over the coupling and end of the pipe until a piece of solder touched to the joint melts into it *(left)*. Remove the flame and hold the solder against the joint, allowing molten solder to be drawn into it by the flux. Continue until the joint is sealed completely by a uniform bead of solder.

SUBSTITUTING CPVC PIPE

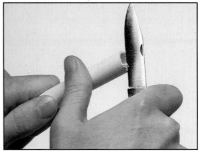

1 **Cut off the damaged pipe,** then ream and file burrs off the ends of the standing pipe. Mark the replacement pipe to length *(above, left)*, then cut it with a backsaw and miter box *(above right, top)*. With a knife, deburr both the inside and outside of each end of the replacement pipe *(above right, bottom)*.

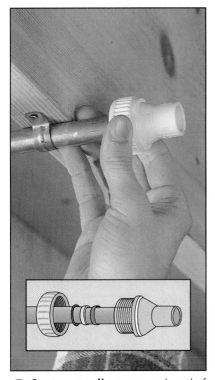

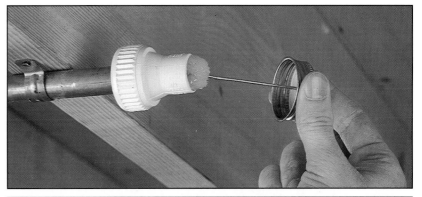

2 **Seat a coupling** onto each end of the standing pipe *(above)*, pushing until the end of the pipe bottoms out inside the coupling's socket *(inset)*. Hand-tighten the couplings.

3 **Coat the contact surfaces** of the couplings and replacement pipe with primer, then a layer of cement *(above, top)*. Working quickly—the adhesive will set in less than 30 seconds—push the standing pipes apart and fit the ends of the replacement pipe into the couplings *(above, bottom)*. Twist the pipe a quarter-turn to spread the cement evenly. **CAUTION:** Ventilate the work area thoroughly.

4 Adding a Bathroom Vanity

💲 Estimated Savings: $105

BEFORE YOU START

◆ Choose a vanity that is big enough to cover holes left by the mounting bracket of an existing sink. For ease of installation and maintenance, select a preformed countertop sink.

◆ Disconnect supply and drain fittings before removing an old sink. Before installing the vanity, do any planned tiling, wallpapering or painting. Remove baseboard and molding behind the vanity so that it will sit against the wall.

Removing a Sink

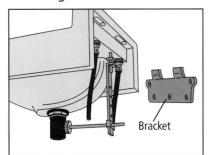

Bracket

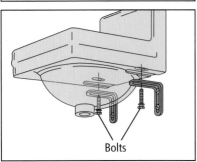

Bolts

Dismount a wall-hung basin by lifting it off the mounting bracket *(above, top)* or removing the bolts *(above, bottom)*.

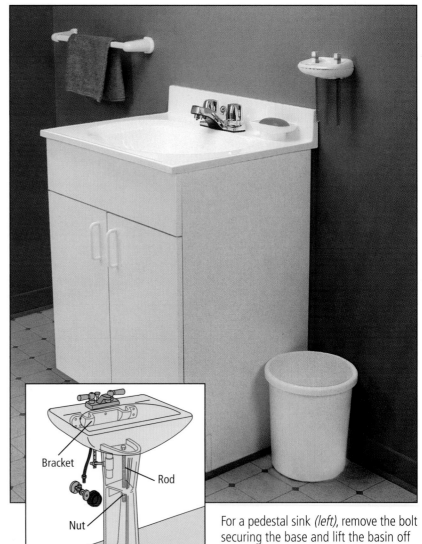

Bracket

Rod

Nut

Bolt

For a pedestal sink *(left)*, remove the bolt securing the base and lift the basin off the mounting bracket. (A threaded rod and nut may join the basin and base.)

WHAT YOU NEED

Tools
- ✔ Stud finder
- ✔ Carpenter's level
- ✔ Backsaw
- ✔ Electric drill
- ✔ Caulking gun
- ✔ Claw hammer
- ✔ Wrenches

Materials
- ✔ Vanity
- ✔ Wood shims
- ✔ Drywall screws
- ✔ Countertop sink
- ✔ Faucet set
- ✔ Adhesive caulk
- ✔ Scribe and shoe molding
- ✔ Finishing nails

✋ SAFETY FIRST

Turn off the water supply to the sink and open the faucet to drain the supply tubes. Wear safety goggles when drilling and hammering.

1 **Outline the vanity** on the wall, centering it roughly with the drain-pipe and the shutoff valves. Locate and mark the center of studs within the outline *(above)*.

Stud finder

2 **Level the vanity** in position against the wall using a carpenter's level. Insert shims under the vanity to level from side to side *(above, left)*, then behind it to level from front to back *(above, right)*. Mark the shims at the edge of the vanity, then remove them one at a time and trim them to length.

3 **Secure the vanity** by driving drywall screws through the back at marked locations of studs *(above)*. Connect the faucet and as many of the supply and drain fittings as possible to the countertop sink.

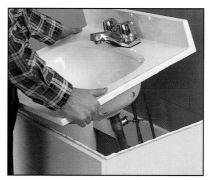

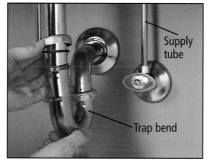

Supply tube

Trap bend

4 **Lay a bead of adhesive** along the top edges of the vanity, then mount the countertop sink *(above, top)*; wipe off excess adhesive immediately. Complete the connecting of supply and drain fittings *(above, bottom)*.

5 **Hide the gap** between each side of the vanity and the wall with prefinished scribe molding *(above)*. Add shoe molding around the base of the vanity.

5 Fixing Faucet Leaks & Drips
$ Estimated Savings: $50

PARTS OF A STEM FAUCET

- CAP
- HANDLE SCREW
- HANDLE
- PACKING NUT
- STEM
- PACKING WASHER
- SEAT WASHER
- WASHER SCREW

BEFORE YOU START

◆ Turn off the shut-off valves below the basin and drain the faucet. If the basin has no valves, turn off the main water valve usually located on the street side of the cellar (see page 221).

◆ If the valves will not close, turn off main valve. Drain the system by opening the faucets at the highest point in the house and working down to the lowest point. This prevents a vacuum from forming.

◆ Plug the drain so faucet parts cannot fall in, and protect the sink with a towel.

◆ As you work, set parts aside in the order removed for easier reassembly.

WHAT YOU NEED

Tools
- ✔ Screwdriver
- ✔ Vise
- ✔ Adjustable wrench
- ✔ Flashlight
- ✔ Pliers
- ✔ Long-nose pliers
- ✔ Seat wrench
- ✔ Hex wrench

Materials
- ✔ Electrician's tape
- ✔ Steel wool

SAFETY FIRST

Locate the main shutoff valve before beginning, so you know where it is in case of an emergency. (See "Shutting off the water supply" on page 221 for further directions.)

REPAIRING A STEM FAUCET

1 **If the spout drips,** repair both hot and cold faucets. Remove any decorative cap. Remove the screw that attaches the handle to the stem *(above)* and pull straight up. If it is wedged on tight, protect the basin or base plate and pry the handle off with a screwdriver.

2 **Unscrew the packing nut** with an adjustable wrench *(above)*. (If the stem comes out with the nut, protect the stem with electrical tape and separate them by clamping the assembly in a vise and removing the nut with a wrench.)

3 **Try to unscrew the stem** by hand *(above)*. Should that fail, set the handle on the stem and turn it in the direction you would to turn on the water. If the stem does not unscrew, it may be a diaphragm or cartridge type; see page 20.

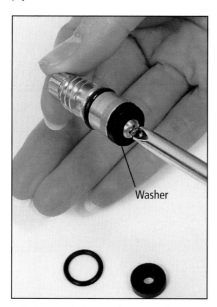

Washer

4 **Inspect the rubber washer** for wear. If the washer is grooved, pitted, frayed or cracked, remove the screw (turn counter-clockwise) and the old washer. Clean the washer seat and stem by rubbing with steel wool. Install a new washer of the same size. Replace a damaged screw with a new one.

5 **Check the valve seats** for signs of wear—scratches, pits, or an uneven surface. Use a flashlight to look inside the faucet body, then run a fingertip around the edge. If scored or pitted, the surface must be replaced or reground using a redressing tool.

FREEING A HANDLE

A stubborn handle can be freed with a faucet-handle puller *(below)* without marring the finish. Insert the center shaft into the hole on the handle, and fit the puller arms under it. Turn the puller handle clockwise to lift the faucet handle off.

CARTRIDGE STEM FAUCET

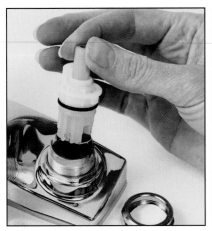

Lift the cartridge out of the faucet *(above, left)*. Note the alignment of the stop and how the keys fit into slots on the sides of the faucet body. With long-nose pliers lift out the washer and spring *(above, right)*. Replace them by pushing the new ones in with a finger. Replace the handle. If the faucet still drips replace the cartridge too.

DIAPHRAGM STEM

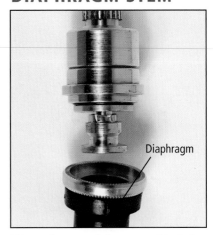

Wrap the top of the stem with cloth and pull out with pliers, or pry it out with a screwdriver. Clean out any broken pieces. Fit a new diaphragm over the bottom of the stem. Reassemble the stem, packing nut and handle.

SINGLE LEVER CARTRIDGE FAUCETS

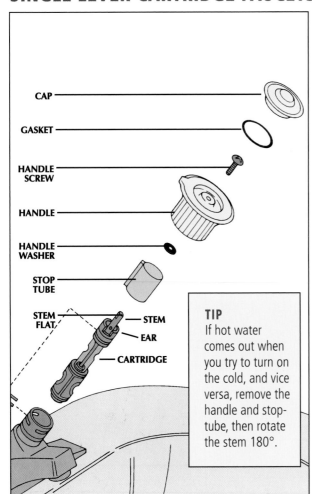

TIP
If hot water comes out when you try to turn on the cold, and vice versa, remove the handle and stop-tube, then rotate the stem 180°.

1 Pry off the cap and its gasket. Unscrew the handle and remove it along with its washer and stop tube. Before removing the cartridge note the orientation of the flat side of the stem and the "ears" near it, so you can position the new one the same way. A retainer clip holds the cartridge in the body. Pull it out with pliers and lift out the cartridge.

2 Hold the new one by its ears and slip it in to position aligned with the slots in the body. Slide the retainer clip through the slots. Turn the stem flats to the same position as they were on the old one. Reassemble the handle.

SINGLE LEVER CERAMIC

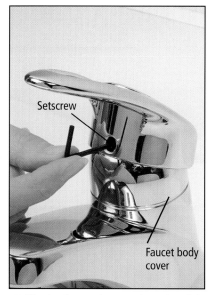

Setscrew

Faucet body cover

1 **If a leak persists,** replace the disk cartridge. Turn off the water and drain the faucet. Raise the lever as high as it can go. Unscrew the setscrew under the lever and remove the handle.

2 **Unscrew the bolts** that hold the disk cartridge in place *(above)*. Remove the cartridge. Take the old one with you to purchase an identical replacement.

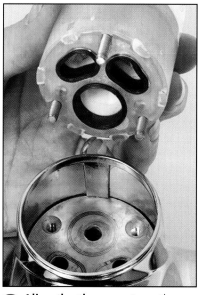

3 **Align the three ports** on the bottom of the new disk cartridge with the three holes in the base of the faucet body. Reassemble the disk cartridge bolts, body cover, and handle.

SINGLE LEVER BALL

Cam assembly

Ball unit

1 **If a ball faucet drips,** replace the two rubber valve seats and springs. Remove the handle by loosening the set screw, but do not remove the screw; it is easily lost. Unscrew the cap assembly and lift it out by its stem; the cam assembly will come out with it. Replace the ball if it is rough or corroded.

2 **Remove the valve seats** and spring with long-nose pliers. Buy a replacement kit and push replacements firmly in place with a fingertip.

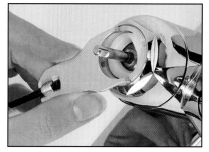

3 **Reposition the ball** and cam assembly into the cavity. Screw on the cap assembly. Turn on the water. Move the ball's stem to the ON position. If water leaks out around the stem, tighten the adjustment ring with a tool provided by the manufacturer or a small screwdriver.

6 Installing a Double-handle Faucet Set
$ Estimated Savings: $60

BEFORE YOU START

◆ Buy a faucet set that fits the spacing of the basin's holes. Determine the spacing by measuring between centers of the existing faucet's handles.

◆ Several hours before removing an existing faucet set, spray the threaded connections with penetrating lubricant.

◆ Clean off crusty deposits under an old faucet set with a solution of equal parts white vinegar and water.

Removing a Faucet Set

To free the pop-up plug mechanism, use pliers to loosen the setscrew securing the lift rod to the clevis (*above, left*). From above the basin, pull out the lift rod. With a basin wrench, unscrew the coupling nuts (*above, right*) to disconnect the supply tubes, then unscrew the locknuts securing the faucet to the basin.

WHAT YOU NEED

Tools
✔ Basin wrench
✔ Adjustable wrench
Materials
✔ Double-handle faucet set
✔ Plumbing tape
✔ Flexible supply tubes

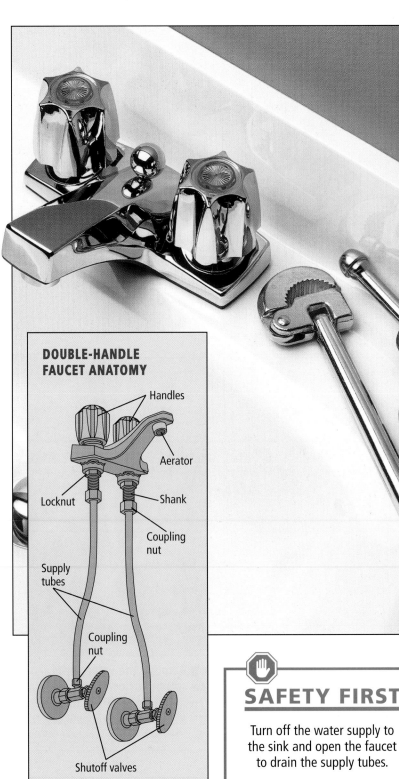

DOUBLE-HANDLE FAUCET ANATOMY

SAFETY FIRST

Turn off the water supply to the sink and open the faucet to drain the supply tubes.

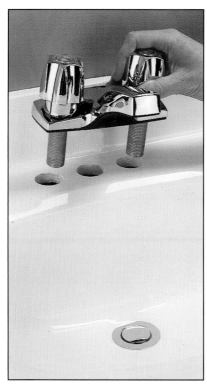

1 **Slip the gasket** and the bottom plate into place on the base of the faucet. Insert the shanks into the holes of the basin *(above)*.

2 **Working below the basin,** thread locknuts onto the shanks *(above)* and hand-tighten them.

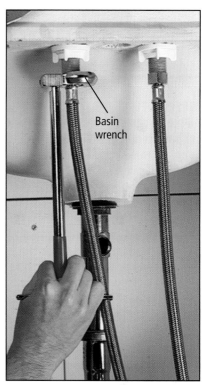

Basin wrench

3 **Wrap the threads** of the shanks with plumbing tape. Insert new rubber washers into the supply tubes. Thread them tightly on the shanks.

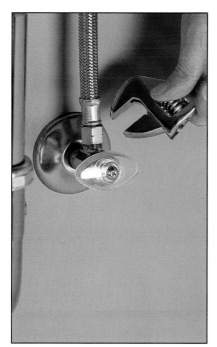

4 **Connect the supply tubes** to the shutoff valves using plumbing tape and washers. With an adjustable wrench, tighten each coupling nut a final half-turn *(above)*.

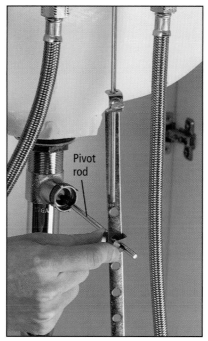

Pivot rod

5 **Assemble the pop-up plug** mechanism, securing the pivot rod to the clevis with a spring clip *(above)*. (To adjust the mechanism, move the pivot rod to a different clevis hole.)

6 **Turn on the water** supply and check for leaks; tighten any loose connections. To flush out sediment, unscrew the aerator *(above)* and open the faucet.

7 Servicing a Water Heater

$ Estimated Savings: $120

BEFORE YOU START

◆ Routine annual procedures can help to avoid problems with a water heater. Drain a few gallons of water from the tank to flush out sediment. Check the drain valve for leaks and test the relief valve—an important safety device that prevents explosion of the tank if water temperature or pressure rises too high.

◆ Reduce energy consumption of a water heater by setting the thermostat control so that water is heated only to the temperature required for efficient operation of major appliances such as dishwashers and clothes washers. Also insulate hot-water supply pipes to help water retain heat.

◆ When a gas water heater doesn't heat water, the problem is most often because the pilot will not stay lit; typically, the solution is to replace the thermocouple—a safety device that shuts off gas automatically when the pilot flame goes out.

◆ One of the most common problems with an electric water heater is a faulty heating element. If the water produced is warm but not hot, suspect that the upper element is faulty; if the water runs hot for a short time and then cold, the lower element is probably faulty.

◆ Make sure that replacement components match the specifications of the water heater. Check the tank for a nameplate that lists the information needed or take along the old parts when purchasing new ones.

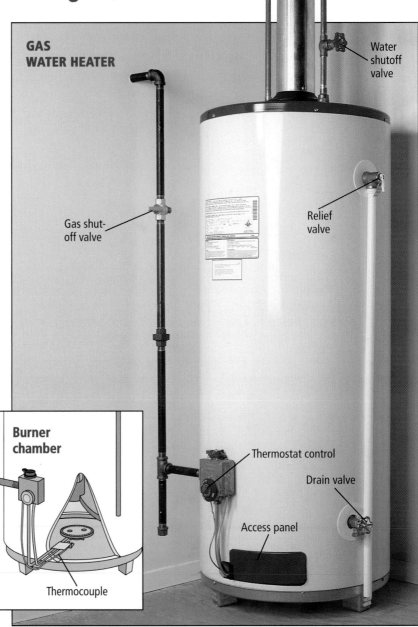

GAS WATER HEATER

Water shutoff valve

Gas shut-off valve

Relief valve

Thermostat control

Drain valve

Access panel

Burner chamber

Thermocouple

SHUTTING OFF GAS

To stop the flow of gas to the water heater, turn the handle of the shutoff valve fully perpendicular to the supply pipe *(right)*.

SAFETY FIRST

Shut off the gas and the water supply when instructed for repairs and allow several hours for water in the tank to cool.

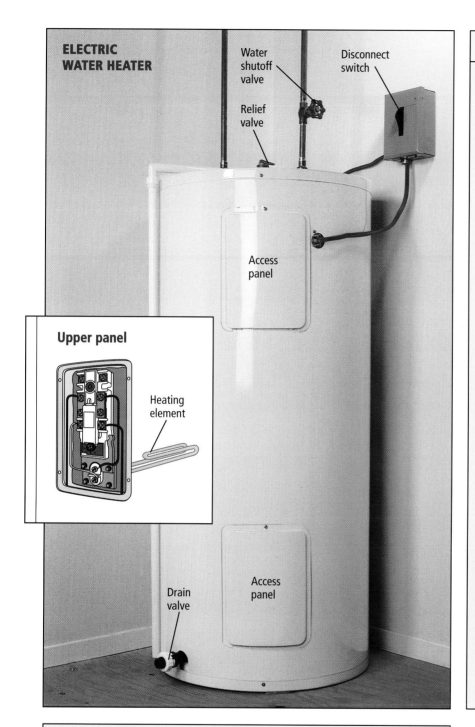

ELECTRIC WATER HEATER

Water shutoff valve

Relief valve

Disconnect switch

Access panel

Upper panel

Heating element

Drain valve

Access panel

WHAT YOU NEED

WHAT YOU NEED

ROUTINE MAINTENANCE
Materials
- ✔ Bucket or garden hose
- ✔ Insulating tubes
- ✔ Duct tape

REPLACING RELIEF VALVE OR DRAIN VALVE
Tools
- ✔ Adjustable wrench
- ✔ Pipe wrench

Materials
- ✔ Replacement relief valve
- ✔ Replacement drain valve and adapter coupling
- ✔ Plumbing tape

REPLACING THERMOCOUPLE
(Gas water heater)
Tools
- ✔ Open-ended wrenches
- ✔ Long-nose pliers

Materials
- ✔ Replacement thermocouple

REPLACING HEATING ELEMENTS
(Electric water heater)
Tools
- ✔ Voltage tester
- ✔ Screwdriver
- ✔ Continuity tester
- ✔ Open-ended wrench

Materials
- ✔ Replacement heating element and gasket

SHUTTING OFF ELECTRICITY

Shut off the electricity to the water heater by flipping the unit disconnect switch to OFF *(right)*. (If there is no disconnect switch, shut off power to the circuit at the service panel.)

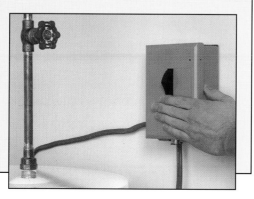

SAFETY FIRST

Shut off the electricity and the water supply when instructed for repairs and allow several hours for water in the tank to cool. Confirm that the electricity is shut off using a voltage tester.

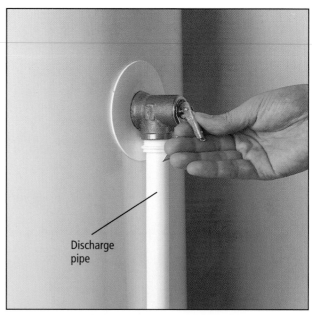

Discharge pipe

Draining the tank. Shut off the gas or electricity and the water supply, then let the tank water cool. Set a bucket under the drain valve and open it *(above)*. Or, connect a garden hose to the valve and run it to a floor drain. If the valve clogs, turn on the water supply for a few minutes to flush out sediment.

Testing the relief valve. Set a bucket under the discharge pipe, then lift up the valve's spring lever for a few seconds *(above)*. **Caution:** Stay clear of the pipe as hot water escapes. Lift up the lever again to clear sediment; if more or less than $\frac{1}{2}$ to 1 cup of water is released at a time, replace the valve.

Adjusting water temperature. Set the thermostat control so that water is heated to about 120°F *(above)*. (To reach the thermostat controls on an electric heater, remove the access panels.)

Insulating hot-water pipes. Shut off the gas or electricity. With a utility knife, trim preslit insulating tubes to the lengths necessary to fit around exposed hot-water supply pipes. Wrap the tubes around the pipes *(above)*, then seal the seams and joints with duct tape.

REPLACING THE RELIEF VALVE

1 **Drain the tank** to a level below the relief valve, then disconnect the discharge pipe using an adjustable wrench *(above)*.

2 **With a pipe wrench,** unscrew the relief valve from the tank *(above)*. Apply firm pressure without jerking to avoid damaging the tank.

3 **Wrap the threads** of a replacement relief valve with plumbing tape, then screw it in *(above)* and tighten it. Reconnect the discharge pipe.

REPLACING THE DRAIN VALVE

1 **Drain the tank,** then unscrew the drain valve if it is metal with a pipe wrench *(above, top)*. To remove a plastic drain valve, turn the control ring by hand counterclockwise, then pull on the handle and turn the ring clockwise *(above, bottom)*— for the number of turns, check the manufacturer's instructions.

2 **Wrap plumbing tape** onto the threads of any adapter coupling needed to fit a new drain valve, then screw it in and tighten it a quarter turn *(above, left)*. Tape the threads of the new valve and screw it into the coupling, then tighten it so that it faces the floor *(above, right)*.

REPLACING THE GAS THERMOCOUPLE

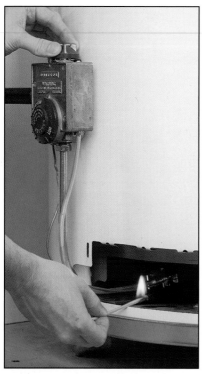

1 **Remove the access panel** and try to relight the pilot. If the pilot fails to stay lit, turn the control knob to OFF and shut off the gas.

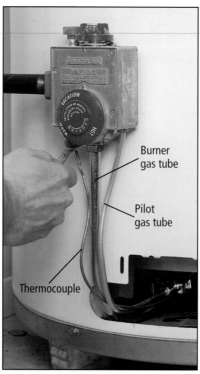

Burner gas tube

Pilot gas tube

Thermocouple

2 **With a wrench,** disconnect the thermocouple, the pilot gas tube and the burner gas tube from the control unit *(above)*.

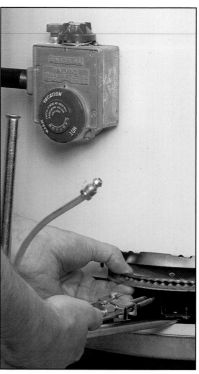

3 **Pull the burner** free of its mounting bracket and slide it out of the chamber *(above)*.

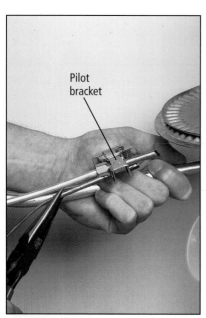

Pilot bracket

4 **Slide the thermocouple** off the pilot bracket, then snap a replacement into place *(above)*.

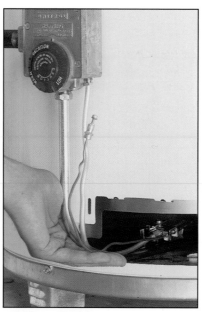

5 **Place the burner** back into the chamber *(above)*, slipping it onto the mounting bracket.

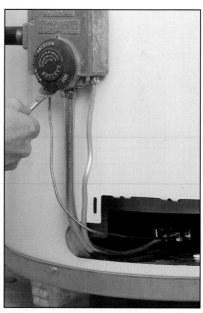

6 **Screw the thermocouple,** pilot gas tube and burner gas tube onto the control unit and tighten them a quarter turn with a wrench *(above)*.

REPLACING ELECTRIC HEATING ELEMENTS

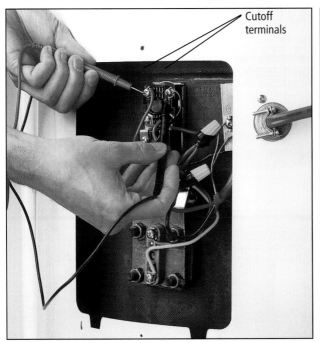

Cutoff terminals

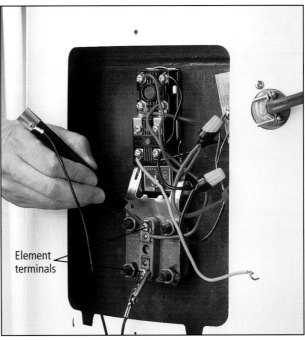

Element terminals

1 **Shut off the electricity** and remove the upper access panel, then confirm that the power is off by touching the probes of a voltage tester to the top pair of high-limit cutoff terminals *(above, left)*. To test the heating element, disconnect one of its wires and touch the probes of a continuity tester to the terminals *(above, right)*. If the tester doesn't light, replace the element *(Step 2)*. Remove the lower access panel to test the other heating element for continuity.

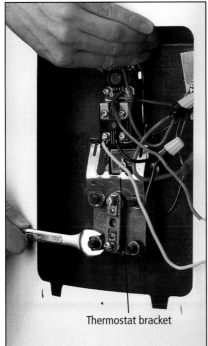

Thermostat bracket

Gasket

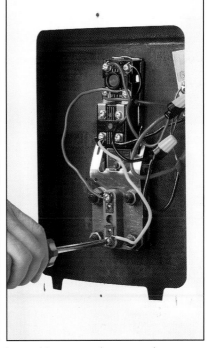

2 **To replace a heating element,** drain the tank. Then, disconnect the element's wires and remove the nuts from the mounting bolts *(above, left)*. Set aside the thermostat bracket and slide out the element *(above, center)*. Fit a new gasket onto the opening and insert a replacement element, then reposition the thermostat bracket and tighten the nuts onto the mounting bolts uniformly a little at a time. Connect the wires to the element's terminals *(above, right)*.

8 Mounting Smoke Detectors

💲 Estimated Savings: $30

BEFORE YOU START

◆ Install at least one smoke detector in a central area on each floor of the house as well as at sites where fires normally start—kitchen, garage and any room with a fireplace.

◆ Local fire departments often provide inspections and give advice on locating smoke detectors free of charge.

Avoiding Dead Air Spaces

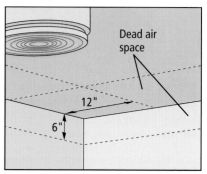

Dead air space

12"

6"

Smoke from a fire rarely circulates to the corners of rooms. Locate a smoke detector on the ceiling at least 12 inches from the walls or on a wall no less than 6 inches from the ceiling.

WHAT YOU NEED

Tools
✔ Stepladder
✔ Electric drill
✔ Screwdriver

Materials
✔ Smoke detector kit
✔ Battery

BATTERY-POWERED SMOKE DETECTORS

Photoelectric
Responds to smoldering fire; less prone to false alarms.

Built-in light
Illuminates escape route when sounds.

Ionization
Responds to hot fire with little smoke.

SAFETY FIRST

Wear safety goggles when operating an electric drill.

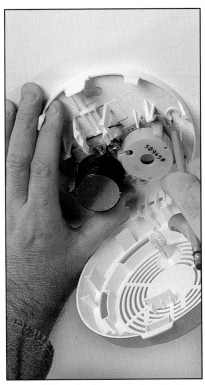

1 **Position the base** and mark the location of screw holes on the surface with a pencil *(above)*.

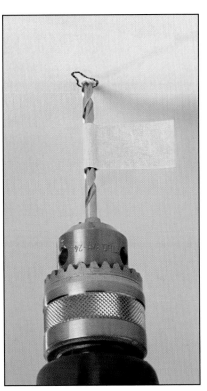

2 **Drill holes** for anchors at the marks *(above)*. As a depth guide, wrap the bit with masking tape.

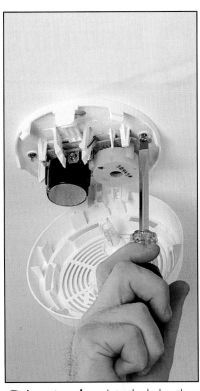

3 **Insert anchors** into the holes, then screw the base into place *(above)*.

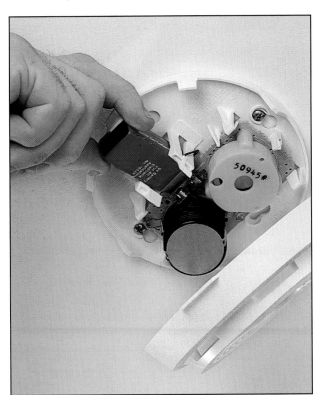

4 **Slide a battery** into the clips on the base *(above)* and close the cover. Push the test button to check that the detector functions.

ROUTINE MAINTENANCE

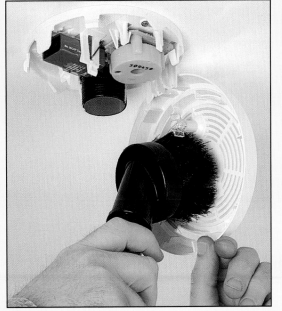

Test smoke detectors monthly. Clear dust from the vents with a vacuum *(above)*, and wipe interior and exterior surfaces clean using a damp cloth. Change the battery at least once every six months.

9 Installing a CO Detector
💲 Estimated Savings: $35

BEFORE YOU START

◆ Carbon monoxide (CO) is a colorless, odorless and potentially fatal gas. It can build up inside a home, especially in winter, from improperly vented furnaces, fireplaces, wood-burning stoves and kerosene heaters.

◆ If you install only one CO detector in your home, it should be near the bedrooms. In a multi-level home, you should install at least one on each level where you can hear the alarms from the bedrooms. Avoid drafty areas where air from outside may result in inaccurate readings. Do not install the unit in the "dead air" space within a half foot of the ceiling.

◆ Do not install alarms in the rooms containing the most common sources of CO. Cars and appliances powered by engines or natural gas often release brief bursts of CO which would result in nuisance alarms. Dirt and grease in basements, garages, and kitchens may coat the detector's sensor and prevent it from functioning.

◆ For more help attaching a unit to a wall see *Hanging Frames on Different Walls* (page 86).

CARBON MONOXIDE DETECTORS

Different models have varying features and prices to match. The simplest and least expensive are similar in appearance and sophistication to a smoke detector. More expensive models may have a digital display to give you a constant reading of CO levels, or a "peak level" button to allow you to check the highest level recorded by the sensor since the last time the unit was unplugged or reset.

Plug-in unit with digital display
Display shows current CO levels as parts per million reading. It is also available as a power cord unit, for mounting at eye level or out of the reach of children.

Simple battery-powered alarm model
Alarm sounds when CO rises to unsafe levels.

WHAT YOU NEED

Tools
✔ Electric drill
✔ Screwdriver
Materials
✔ Carbon monoxide detector kit

SAFETY FIRST

Wear safety goggles when operating an electric drill.

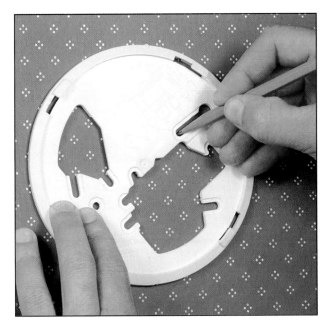

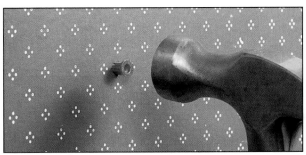

1 **Mark screw holes** using the removable back of the unit as a template. One screw hole is an adjustable "keyhole" *(above)*. Some units plug directly into a wall outlet. Others are mounted on the wall, but plug in from a cord.

2 **Drill holes at marks.** If drilling on a hollow wall, insert a plastic anchor in each hole *(above, top)*. To mount the keyhole opening, insert the screw until the head is about $\frac{1}{8}$ inch from the wall *(above, bottom)*.

3 **Position the back** with the keyhole opening over its screw. Line up the other opening and drive in the screw *(above, top)*. Insert the battery into the unit (some also have a separate sensor to insert) and twist the unit onto its base.

ROUTINE MAINTENANCE

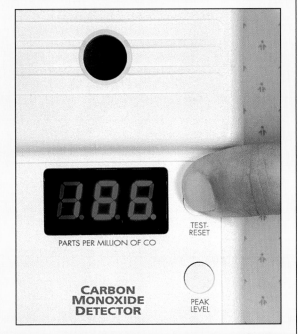

Test your unit once a week by pressing the test button. (Cover the unit's alarm hole; the decibel level can be jarring.) This unit is about to register its highest level. The maximum allowable concentration of CO in the air is 50 ppm (parts per million) over eight hours.

10 Mounting a Ceiling Fan
💲 Estimated Savings: $90

BEFORE YOU START

Be sure to choose a suitable location for installing a ceiling fan:

◆ Blades must be at least 7 feet off the floor and have 2 feet of clearance from obstructions.

◆ Never mount a fan at a spot where it might get wet.

◆ To best support a fan's weight, the electrical box should be mounted on a bar hanger secured to joists.

ADDING CEILING SUPPORT

Reinforce an electrical box secured to a single joist with a screw-type bar hanger *(right)*. The bar slips into the opening in the ceiling and is extended between two joists, then the box is hung from it with a U-bolt and nuts.

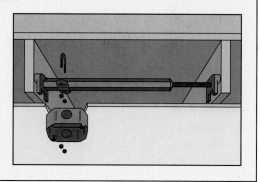

WHAT YOU NEED

Tools
✔ Screwdriver
✔ Box wrench
Materials
✔ Ceiling fan

SAFETY FIRST

Shut off electricity to the circuit at the service panel. Confirm that the electricity has been shut off using a voltage tester.

1 Remove the mounting screws of the existing fixture and unscrew the wire caps *(above)*. Disconnect the wires after confirming that the power is shut off.

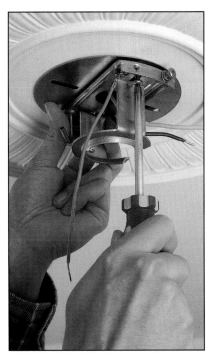

2 Slip the wires from the electrical box through the opening in the fan's ceiling plate, then screw the plate to the box *(above)*. (The plate's green wire will ground the fan to the box.)

3 Feed the fan's wires and the security line through the canopy and downpipe *(above)*. Thread the downpipe into the housing and tighten its setscrew.

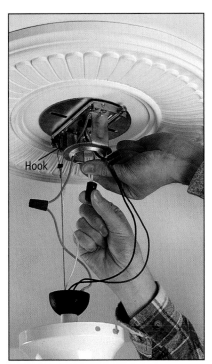

4 Hang the fan by its security line on the ceiling plate's hook, then join the wires: green to green (ground); black and blue—or other fourth color—to black; white to white *(above)*.

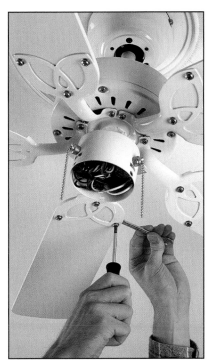

5 Screw the canopy to the ceiling plate. Secure the blades to the support brackets with the fasteners provided *(above)*. **Caution:** Don't operate the fan until the blades are attached.

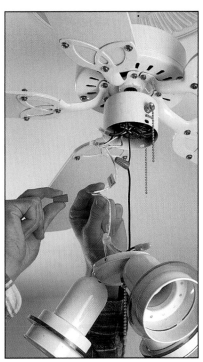

6 Connect the wires of the fan's light fixture: black to black; white to white *(above)*. Screw the fixture to the housing. (If not installing a light fixture, substitute a cover plate.)

11 Installing a Dimmer Switch
💲 Estimated Savings: $35

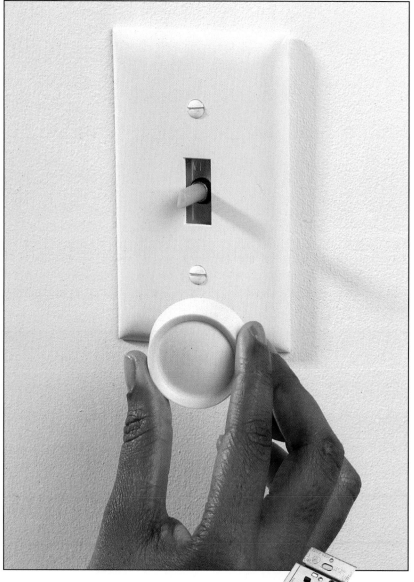

BEFORE YOU START

◆ Add a conventional dimmer switch only to control incandescent lighting. Dimmer control of fluorescent lighting is possible, but calls for a special switch with a different installation procedure. Appliances and power tools plugged into an outlet controlled by a dimmer switch will be severely damaged.

◆ Install a dimmer switch of a suitable wattage rating—higher than the total of the lighting to be controlled, but within the limits specified on the electrical box. Connect any green lead on the switch to the box grounding screw.

WHAT YOU NEED

Tools
✔ Screwdriver
Materials
✔ Dimmer switch
✔ Wire caps

✋ SAFETY FIRST

Shut off electricity to the circuit at the service panel. Confirm that the electricity has been shut off using a voltage tester.

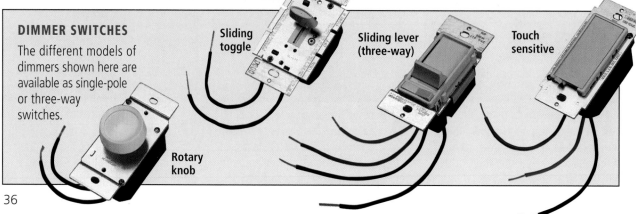

DIMMER SWITCHES

The different models of dimmers shown here are available as single-pole or three-way switches.

Sliding toggle

Sliding lever (three-way)

Touch sensitive

Rotary knob

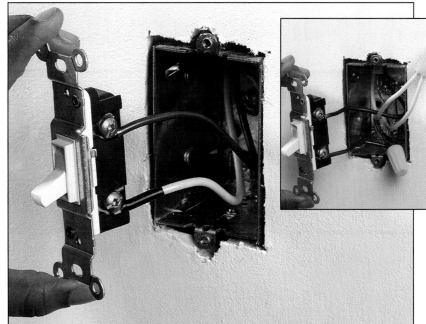

1 **Unscrew the cover plate** and confirm that the power is shut off before touching the wires. Remove the screws from the mounting strap *(above)* and pull out the switch.

2 **Count the cables** entering the electrical box. If there is one cable, a black wire and a white wire are connected to the switch *(above)*; the white wire should be recoded black, as shown, with electrical tape. If there is more than one cable, two black wires are secured to the switch and the white wires are joined with a wire cap *(inset)*. Remove the wires from the switch by loosening the screw terminals with a screwdriver.

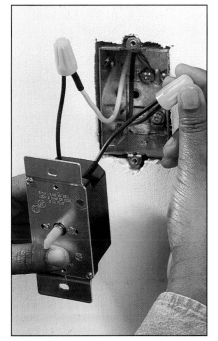

3 **Join the leads** of the dimmer switch to the wires in the box with wire caps; tug each connection gently *(above)* to check that it is secure. Mount the switch in the box and screw on the cover plate.

THREE-WAY SWITCH

One three-way switch in a three- or four-way series may be replaced by a three-way dimmer switch. Before removing the wires from the existing switch, mark the common wire—secured to the black or darkest terminal—with masking tape *(right, top)*. Join the common lead of the dimmer switch to the marked wire *(right, bottom)*, then connect each of the other leads to one of the remaining wires in the box.

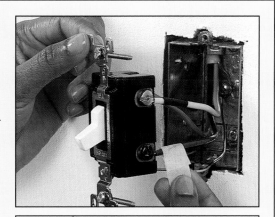

12 Installing a GFCI Outlet
💲 Estimated Savings: $35

BEFORE YOU START

◆ Building codes specify that a new outlet must be protected by a ground-fault circuit interrupter (GFCI) if it is installed in a bathroom, in a kitchen above a countertop within 6 feet of a sink, in an unfinished basement, in a garage, or outdoors. For safety, replace existing standard outlets at these locations with GFCI outlets.

◆ A GFCI outlet protects all outlets after it on the circuit. To check if an outlet is first on the circuit, turn off the power and wrap electrical tape around each wire, then restore power and plug a working lamp into each other outlet on the circuit. If no other outlet works, the outlet is first on the circuit.

Exterior GFCI Outlet
A GFCI outlet is made weather-proof for outdoor use by a heavy cover and a spring-loaded door.

WHAT YOU NEED

Tools
- ✔ Screwdriver
- ✔ Long-nose pliers
- ✔ Voltage tester

Materials
- ✔ GFCI outlet

✋ SAFETY FIRST

Shut off electricity to the circuit at the service panel. Confirm that the electricity has been shut off using a voltage tester.

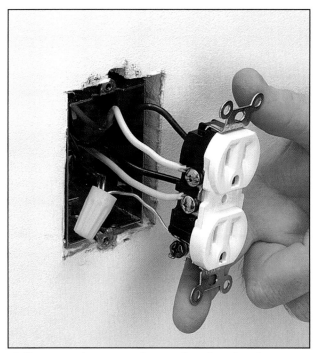

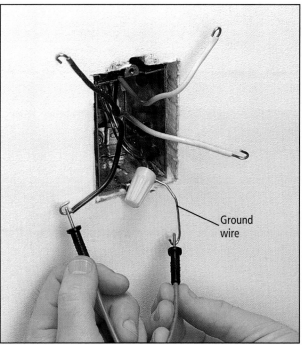

Ground wire

1 **Unscrew the cover plate** and confirm that the power is shut off before touching the wires. Remove the screws from the mounting strap and pull out the outlet *(above)*, then disconnect the wires from it.

2 **Isolate each wire,** then restore the power. Touch one probe of a voltage tester to the ground wire and the other probe to each black wire *(above)*. Note the wire that causes the tester to light, then shut off the power and tag it. **CAUTION:** Don't make hand contact with live wires.

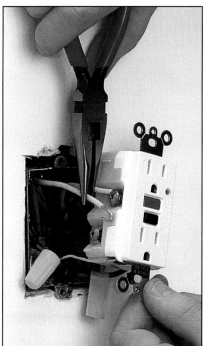

GFCI TESTING

3 **Connect the ground wire** to the GFCI outlet's green terminal screw, then secure the black wires to brass screws and the white wires to silver screws: the tagged wire and the wire in the same cable to the LINE terminals; the other pair of wires to the LOAD terminals *(above, left)*. Mount the outlet in the box *(above, right)* and screw on the cover plate.

Press the TEST button *(above)*. If the wiring is correct, the RESET button will pop out, interrupting power to the outlet. Press the RESET button to restore power.

13 Replacing a Lamp Socket
$ Estimated Savings: $15

SOCKET ANATOMY

- Outer shell
- Insulating sleeve
- Socket
- Terminal screw
- Cap
- Setscrew

SOCKETS WITH SWITCHES
The types of sockets shown here are interchangeable.

Push lever

Twist knob

Pull chain

BEFORE YOU START
Be certain that the socket is causing the problem:
- ◆ Change the bulb and try the lamp in a different outlet.
- ◆ Check if the plug is loose or damaged and if the cord is cracked or split.

Adjusting the Contact Tab

Clean the socket's contact tab by scraping it lightly with a small screwdriver, then gently pry the tab upward *(above)* so it protrudes enough to make proper contact with the bulb.

WHAT YOU NEED

Tools
- ✔ Small screwdriver
- ✔ Long-nose pliers
- ✔ Continuity tester

Materials
- ✔ Replacement socket

SAFETY FIRST

Unplug the lamp from the outlet to work on the socket.

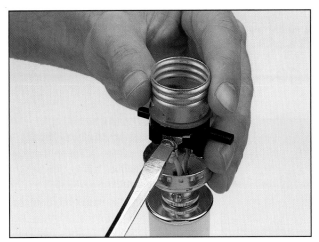

1 **Disassemble the socket** by squeezing at the PRESS markings and twisting off the outer shell. Slip off the insulating sleeve, then loosen the terminal screws *(above)* and disconnect the wires.

2 **Test the socket** for continuity by clipping one tester probe to the metal base and touching the other probe to the silver (neutral) terminal screw *(above)*. If the tester doesn't light, replace the socket *(Step 4)*.

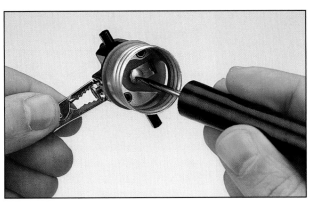

3 **Test the switch** for continuity by clipping one tester probe to the brass terminal screw and touching the other probe to the contact tab *(above)*. The tester should light only when the switch is turned ON.

THREE-WAY SWITCH

Test for continuity by clipping one tester probe to the brass terminal screw and touching the other probe in turn to the vertical tab *(below)* and the contact tab.

As the switch is turned to each of the three ON settings, the tester should light only when touching the tabs as follows:

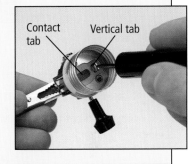

Contact tab   Vertical tab

1   Vertical tab only
2   Contact tab only
3   Both tabs

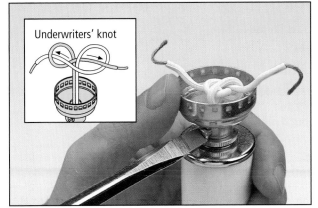

Underwriters' knot

4 **To install a new socket,** first slip the cap onto the cord and tie the wire ends into an Underwriters' knot *(inset)* for strain relief. Tighten the setscrew to secure the cap *(above)*. Twist the strands of each wire together clockwise.

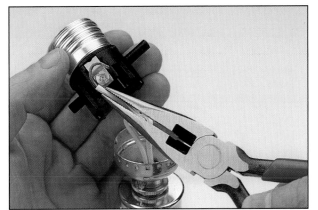

5 **Hook the ridged** or marked (neutral) wire clockwise onto the silver terminal screw and tighten it. Connect the other wire to the brass terminal *(above)*. Slip the insulating sleeve and outer shell into the cap, twisting gently until they snap into place.

14 Insulating an Attic
$ Estimated Savings: $20 per 100 sq. ft.

BEFORE YOU START

◆ Insulation is rated by its resistance to heat flow, or R-value. For an R-value of 19, recommended for most regions, batts 6 inches thick are required.

◆ To estimate how much insulation to buy, multiply the square footage by .90 if joists are spaced at 16-inch intervals; by .94 if spaced at 24-inch intervals.

◆ Place sheets of plywood or boards across joists to use as a walkway.

◆ Light the work area adequately; hang worklights by nails from rafters.

Providing for Air Flow

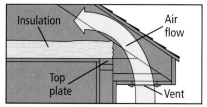

Air flow is needed to prevent moisture buildup that causes rot. Insulate only as far as the top plates of walls below.

WHAT YOU NEED

Tools
✔ Utility knife
✔ Straightedge
✔ Tin snips

Materials
✔ Insulation batts
✔ Light-gauge metal

PLASTIC VAPOR BARRIER

When insulating with a material that doesn't have its own vapor barrier, install a vapor barrier of polyethylene. Cut the plastic into strips a few inches wider than the distance between joists, then staple them in place to the sides of the joists *(left)* without leaving gaps or bulges.

SAFETY FIRST

Wear safety goggles, a dust mask and work gloves when handling fiberglass insulation. Protect your head with a safety helmet.

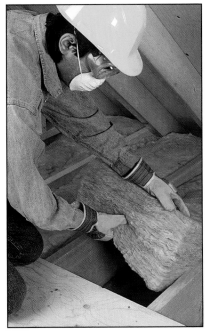

1 **Lay the batts** vapor-barrier side down between joists *(above)*. Place batts far enough against the eaves to cover the top plate without obstructing the flow of air through vents.

2 **Cut batts to fit** using a utility knife. Set the batt on a board and compress it at the cutting line with a straightedge to slice it cleanly *(above)*.

Tin snips

3 **Wrap metal flashing** around the chimney *(above)* to safeguard against fire. Trim batts to fit snugly at the chimney and obstacles. Compress batts to slide them under wires.

2-by-6

4 **Add a second layer** of batts, if necessary, for greater R-value. Slash the vapor barriers of the batts so moisture can escape, then lay them perpendicular to the joists *(above)*. Notched 2-by-6s nailed to the joists and standing 6 inches above them will support a walkway over the second layer.

ATTIC ACCESS
An insulated enclosure built of 2-by-4s and plywood prevents air from descending and rising attic stairs. Lid stops fastened to the frame on the hinged side of the lid *(right, top)* allow it to open without swinging too far; a 2-by-4 secured to the unhinged edge of the lid keeps it from warping. Insulation batts trimmed to fit the frame's sides and lid *(right, bottom)* are held in place by staples driven through their vapor barriers.

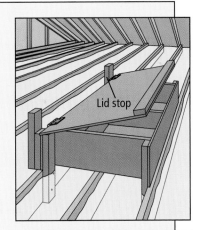

Lid stop

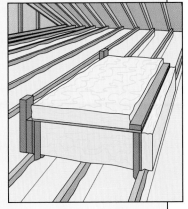

15 Weatherproofing a Door
$ Estimated Savings: $45

Stop

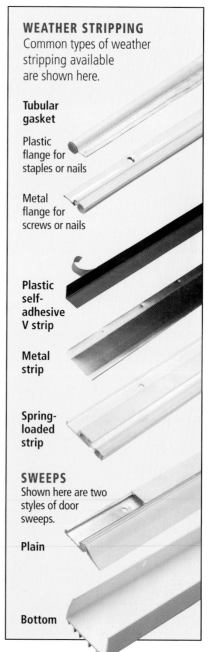

WEATHER STRIPPING
Common types of weather stripping available are shown here.

Tubular gasket

Plastic flange for staples or nails

Metal flange for screws or nails

Plastic self-adhesive V strip

Metal strip

Spring-loaded strip

SWEEPS
Shown here are two styles of door sweeps.

Plain

Bottom

BEFORE YOU START

◆ Select weather stripping and a sweep to suit the door; installation is the same whether the frame has jambs with a stop recess *(above)* or traditional stop *(inset)*.

◆ Cut weather stripping and a sweep carefully to avoid gaps; trim off sections that would cover hardware or otherwise interfere with operation of the door.

◆ Before driving in fasteners all the way, adjust the weather stripping and sweep so that the door opens and closes easily.

WHAT YOU NEED

Tools
✔ Tin snips or hacksaw
✔ Electric drill
✔ Screwdriver
✔ Claw hammer

Materials
✔ Weather stripping
✔ Door sweep

SAFETY FIRST

Wear safety goggles when operating an electric drill.

DOOR FRAMES

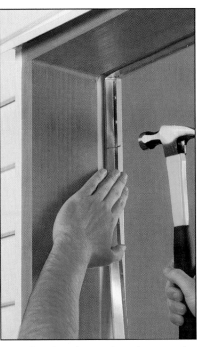

Tubular gasket. With the door closed, position the strips and mark hole locations. Then, open the door to bore pilot holes and drive in screws *(above)*.

Metal strip. Placing the edge opposite to the nailing flange so that it faces the stop, fasten each strip to the jamb with nails *(above)*.

Spring-loaded strip. Set each strip on the jamb *(above)* so that it compresses by a third when the door is closed, then bore pilot holes and screw it into place.

DOOR BOTTOMS

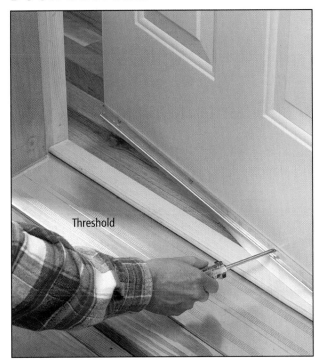

Threshold

Plain sweep. Position the sweep so that it rests against the threshold and allows the door to open and close smoothly, then drill pilot holes and drive in screws *(above)*.

Bottom sweep. Slide the sweep into position *(above)* and close the door to let it drop against the threshold. Then, drill pilot holes and screw the sweep into place.

16 Installing a Motion Detector
💲 Estimated Savings: $60

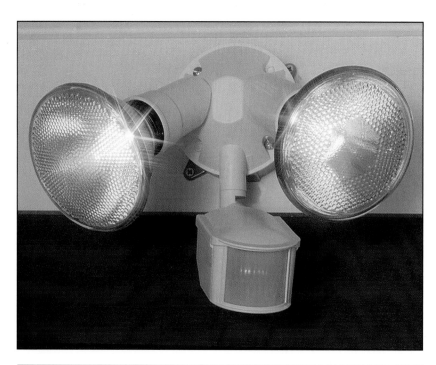

BEFORE YOU START
◆ Make a careful sketch of your house and property, including existing light sources around your home. Use this to determine exactly where you need your motion-detector lights.

◆ Keep in mind that infrared motion detectors work best for detecting movement *across* their path, not toward the sensor. Don't mount the sensor on an unstable object, such as a young tree, or over a heat source, such as a heating vent. Moving objects, like swaying trees or rippling water, in the sensor's direct field of vision may also cause the lights to go on.

TIPS
With motion-activated floodlight units, the lights turn on when the sensor detects movement within its field of vision, which is adjustable. If there is no more movement, the lights turn off after a specified period of time and stay off until triggered again.

◆ If you wish to minimize the detector's response to animals, you can adjust the sensitivity knob; some models also come with blinders you can use to block the sensor's lower field of vision.

◆ The sensitivity knob can also be adjusted to reduce the sensor's range—useful for avoiding unwanted responses to cars or pedestrians passing by the house. Alternatively, rotate the sensor toward the ground.

◆ Don't forget that your motion detector unit comes with an adjustable timer, so that you can vary the length of time the flood-lights stay on once the sensor is triggered (see "Setting the Timing," above left).

SETTING THE TIMING
When movement or heat causes the lights to turn on they will stay on for a set period of time. The factory setting is normally around 6 minutes, but can be adjusted by a switch on the detector. *(right)*.

WHAT YOU NEED

Tools
✔ Screwdriver
✔ Hammer
✔ Voltage tester
✔ Caulking gun

Materials
✔ Motion detector kit
✔ Silicone caulking
✔ Floodlight bulbs

🛑 SAFETY FIRST

Shut off the electricity to the circuit at the service panel. Confirm that the electricity has been shut off using a voltage tester. Be sure to use wires, fixtures, and bulbs designed for outdoor use. When installing the detector and floodlights, watch out for high voltage wires.

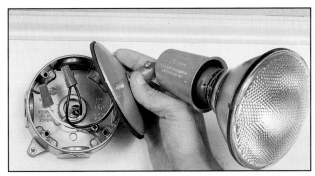

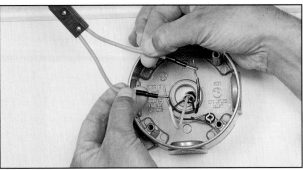

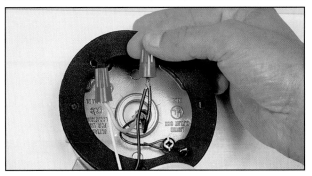

1 **Turn off the power** at the main fuse box. Remove the old floodlight fixture from the outside junction box *(above, top)*. To make sure that the wires are dead use a voltage tester to touch the white and black wires *(above, bottom)*. The bulb will light if the wires are live.

2 **Thread the fixture wires** through the coverplate gasket, and use wire nuts to connect the fixture's white wires with the white supply wires, and the fixture's black wires with the black supply wires. No bare wires should be left exposed. Connect any green or bare ground wire to the junction box.

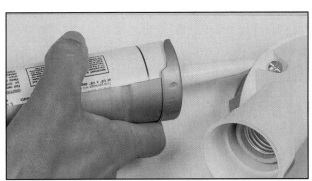

3 **Fold all wires** carefully into the junction box, and screw the fixture onto the box. Fold the rubber gasket that comes with the detector over the threads on the flood light to seal out moisture. Caulk any remaining open screwholes *(above, top)*. Screw in exterior flood lamps.

RUNNING ELECTRICAL SUPPLY TO THE OUTSIDE OF YOUR HOUSE

Most motion detector kits come with instructions assuming you will be installing the floodlight unit to an existing fixture of the sort that is usually found above a garage door. If you do not already have a lighting fixture or outside junction or outlet box in the right spot, you will need to run an electrical supply from an inside junction box.

With the power shut off at the service panel, connect an insulated THHN cable to the house wiring with wire caps; match black wires to black, white to white, and bare ground wire to bare ground wire and to the junction box.

The easiest way to feed the cable from the junction box you're tapping into (most likely in the basement) to the new fixture location is to drill a $1\frac{1}{4}$-inch hole on the outside of the house in the spot you want the new fixture to be mounted. Then, feed an electrician's "snake" down the inside of the wall to a hole you've made in the wall near the existing junction box. Attach the new cable to the snake, and pull it back up and out the hole you've just drilled.

INTERIOR

REPAIRS AND IMPROVEMENTS

PROJECT		PAGE
17	Preparing Surfaces for Paint or Wallpaper	50
18	Painting Interior Walls & Ceilings	54
19	Wallpapering a Room	58
20	Hanging a Wallcovering Border	64
21	Repairing Wallcoverings	68
22	Regrouting Rigid Tiles	72
23	Replacing a Laminate Countertop	74
24	Refacing Cabinets	78
25	Installing Molding & Chair Rails	82
26	Hanging Frames on Different Walls	86
27	Correcting Interior Doors	88
28	Framing an Interior Wall	94
29	Hanging Drywall	98
30	Repairing Drywall Holes	104
31	Repairing Interior Foundation Cracks	106

17 Preparing Surfaces for Paint or Wallpaper

$ Estimated Savings: $180 for 8x10 Room

BEFORE YOU START

◆ If your house was built or painted in 1978 or before, lead and asbestos may be present. See page 219 for precautions.

◆ Washing walls and woodwork with heavy-duty household detergent is sufficient preparation before painting or papering if no scraping, patching or other repairs are needed. Surfaces must be dry before applying the new finish.

SAFETY FIRST

Protect hands from cleaning agents and paint solvents by wearing rubber gloves. Wear safety glasses when applying paint remover and a respirator if the product contains methylene chloride. Make sure there is sufficient ventilation. When sanding, wear a dust mask.

PAINTING OVER PAPER

If it can't be stripped because the wall is fragile or if you want to save time, wallpaper can be painted. Glue down loose edges and corners *(right);* then cover seams and imperfections with thin layers of spackling compound. Sand the patches flush with the paper. Roll on a primer-sealer to prevent wallpaper dyes from bleeding through and to create a surface for holding paint.

WHAT YOU NEED

Tools
- ✔ Putty knives
- ✔ Nail set
- ✔ Hammer
- ✔ Natural bristle paintbrushes
- ✔ Old scissors
- ✔ Long-nose pliers
- ✔ Paring knife

Materials
- ✔ Scrap: 1x3 or 1x4
- ✔ Wood primer
- ✔ Wood filler
- ✔ Wallpaper paste
- ✔ Wallpaper primer-sealer
- ✔ Turpentine
- ✔ Shellac
- ✔ Paint remover
- ✔ Fine- and medium-grit sandpaper

MAKING A SANDING BLOCK

1 **Cut a 4-inch-long piece** of 1-by-3 or 1-by-4. Using old scissors or a utility knife, cut rectangles of different-grit sandpapers big enough to encircle the block. Wrap the paper around the block, grit side out *(above)*.

2 **Hold the sandpaper** firmly in place around the wood, using your index finger to secure the seam *(above)*. When sanding walls, move the sanding block in a circular pattern. On bare wood, move the block with straight strokes, working along the grain.

SANDING DETAILED AREAS

SCRAPING PAINT

To sand intricate spaces, moldings, or window sash muntins, fold the sandpaper into quarters *(above, left)*, creating a sharp sanding edge. Slip the sanding edge into the molding and sand *(above, right)*, following the contours of the wood. Use care when sanding near glass to prevent scratches. Refold the paper frequently to make a fresh sanding edge.

Slide the edge of a putty knife beneath the paint and push to dislodge any peeling flakes. If peeling is excessive *(above)*, feel for dampness that indicates moisture problems.

STRIPPING OLD PAINT

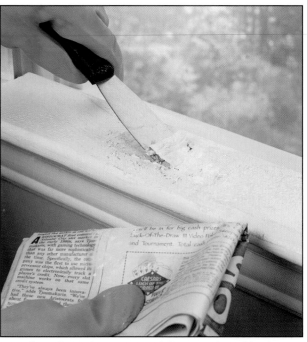

1 **With a clean,** inexpensive paintbrush, coat the paint thickly with remover. Protect surrounding surfaces (including the floor) with newspaper as needed. Fumes are dangerous, so be certain there's sufficient ventilation.

2 **After the paint starts to blister** and wrinkle, skim it off with a 2-inch putty knife. Wipe the blade of the knife on newspaper to clean it. Repeat this procedure as needed to remove all the paint.

PATCHING WOOD KNOTS

If a knot fits tightly in its hole, scrape off hardened resin on the knot with a paring knife. Clean with turpentine, fill any pits or cracks with wood filler, and sand smooth. Prime with thinned shellac before painting.

Remove a loose knot with long-nose pliers and fill the hole with layers of wood filler. Let the filler dry, sand it smooth, and prime with thinned shellac. Then sand lightly again before painting.

COUNTERSINKING NAILS

FILLING HOLES AND CRACKS

To countersink a protruding nail, place the point of a nail set on the nailhead. Strike the nail set with the hammer, embedding the nail about $\frac{1}{8}$ inch below the surface.

1 Use wood filler for nail holes, gouges and cracks in wood. Contour with a putty knife. Add more if needed after first layer has dried.

2 When the filler is dry, sand the area so it is smooth and the filler lays flush with the surrounding woodwork.

3 Brush primer onto the filler, feathering the edges so they will not show under the finish coat.

18 Painting Interior Walls & Ceilings

$ Estimated Savings: $35 per 100 sq. ft.

BEFORE YOU START

◆ Fill holes (see page 104), patch cracks and caulk gaps. Sand repairs smooth and apply a primer-sealer. Wash surfaces with a mild household cleaner and rinse well.

◆ Paint a room's ceiling before the walls. To ensure that the job proceeds smoothly, take the time to prepare properly. Move out furnishings or relocate them to the center and cover them. Drape flooring and other immovables with drop cloths, newspapers, plastic sheeting or masking tape.

Shielding Electrical Fixtures

Shut off power to the room, then take the cover plates off switches and outlets. Loosen a light fixture's canopy and wrap it with plastic *(above)*. Keep the light off until the plastic is removed.

SAFETY FIRST

Keep your hips between the rails of the ladder; don't overreach. Ventilate the work area to minimize the inhalation of paint fumes.

WHAT YOU NEED

Tools
✔ Stepladder
✔ Paintbrush
✔ Roller cover
✔ Roller frame
✔ Extension pole
✔ Roller pan

Materials
✔ Paint

CEILING SURFACES

1 **Cut in along the perimeter** and around openings for fixtures with a 2-inch paintbrush. Make four or five overlapping strokes perpendicular to the edge *(above, left)*, then smooth over them with a parallel stroke *(above, right)*.

2 **Start one brush width** from the corner to cut in along the adjacent edge *(above)*.

3 **Work one section** at a time across the surface to apply paint with a roller and an extension pole. Alternately pushing the roller toward an edge and pulling it back, paint a W pattern about 3 feet square *(above, left)*. Without lowering the roller, crisscross back to fill in the pattern *(above, right)*. Move the roller slowly and apply even pressure, continuing until the entire section is uniformly covered.

1 **Bead in at edges** where adjacent surfaces will not be painted. With a 2-inch paintbrush, press the bristle tips against the surface *(above, left)* until a bead of paint emerges. In one smooth, steady motion, draw the bristle tips to within $\frac{1}{16}$ inch of the edge and along it *(above, right)*—which forces paint just to the edge.

2 **At an inside corner,** press the bristle tips against the surface *(above)* until a bead of paint is forced to the edge.

3 **Cut in along edges** where adjacent surfaces will be painted. Make four or five overlapping strokes perpendicular to the edge *(above, left)*, then smooth over them with a parallel stroke *(above, right)*.

4 **If an adjacent surface** is protected by masking tape, cut in along the edge the same way *(above)*.

5 **Working one section** at a time across the upper surfaces, apply paint with a roller and an extension pole. Alternately push the roller toward the edge and pull it back to paint an M pattern about 3 feet square *(above, left)*. Without lifting the roller, crisscross back to fill in the pattern *(above, right)*. Move the roller slowly and apply even pressure, continuing until the entire section is uniformly covered.

6 **For the lower surfaces,** remove the extension pole from the roller and apply paint to one section at a time the same way *(above)*.

NARROW SURFACES

If a surface's width makes using a roller impractical, fill in with a paintbrush *(above)*. To disguise lapmarks, smooth out the paint with diagonal strokes.

19 Wallpapering a Room
💲 Estimated Savings: $12.50 per single roll

BEFORE YOU START

◆ Wallpaper is pasted on the wall in consecutive strips clockwise or counter-clockwise around the room, with the pattern of each strip matching the previous one. Unless you're covering only part of the room or the room has a floor-to-ceiling interruption on one wall, a mismatch will probably occur along the edge of the last strip. That's why it's important to plan ahead and start the series of strips in a spot least likely to be seen.

◆ If there are already two or more layers of old paper on the wall, if you're hanging a vinyl covering or if the old paper is not sound, remove any old paper first *(see below, left).*

◆ Choose a pattern that matches your room: large prints and dark colors make the room seem smaller; vertical patterns make the ceilings seem higher.

◆ If you're repainting the trim or base-board, do so before repapering.

◆ Wallpaper is sold in single or double rolls. Take the measurements of your room with you when you go to the wallpaper store.

REMOVING OLD WALLPAPER

To remove coverings that were made to be removed, lift a corner of the covering at the top of a section with a utility knife. Carefully peel the covering downward, pulling it flat against itself to minimize ripping of the paper backing. Remove any backing that remains stuck to the wall, but leave the fuzzy residue to help the new wall covering adhere.

Three ways to remove nonstrippable paper:

1. Rent a wallpaper steamer from a wallpaper dealer. Saturate the paper by holding the flat metal pan against the wall. Scrape off the paper.

2. Commercial wallpaper-removing liquids are sold by wallpaper dealers, but first test the paper by spraying a little water on it. If the water does not penetrate, perforate the paper with a scraper blade or perforating tool.

3. If waterproof adhesive was used to apply the wall covering it must be removed with a wall scraper. Hold the blade of the scraper perpendicular to the wall and slit the paper horizontally. Apply gentle pressure to avoid damaging the wallboard. Slide the blade into a slit at an angle, loosen one section of paper at a time, and tear the loosened sections off with your fingers.

WHAT YOU NEED

Tools
✔ Broad putty knife
✔ Chalk line or carpenter's level
✔ Seam roller
✔ Smoothing brush
✔ Paste brush
✔ Utility knife
✔ Scissors
✔ Paste bucket
✔ Tape measure

Materials
✔ Wall sizing
✔ Wallpaper
✔ Wallpaper paste

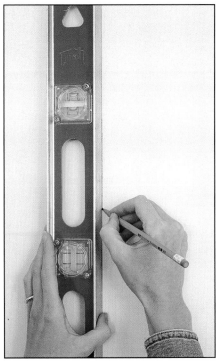

SNAPPING A CHALK LINE

Tack the end of a chalk line high on the wall; when the case stops swinging, pull it slightly downward until the string is taut, press it firmly against the wall, and snap the string *(above)*.

1 **Apply sizing** (a type of glue) to the entire surface area with a roller *(above, left)*. To begin papering, measure the width of the wallpaper roll minus 1 inch from an inconspicuous corner. Drop a chalk line at this spot or use a level *(above, right)* to mark a true vertical line.

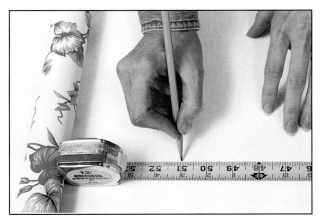

2 **Measure the height** of the wall from the baseboard to the ceiling. Mark off this distance plus 4 inches on the roll of wallpaper *(above)* and cut the first strip this length.

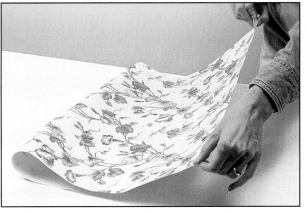

3 **Apply paste evenly** with a brush to the face-down strip, starting at the top. Double over a quarter of the paper's length from the top end so the pasted side touches itself *(above)*. Do not crease or press the folded edge.

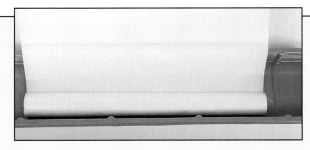

PRE-PASTED PAPER

Often papers are now made with a coating of dry paste already applied. Roll the cut strip, paste side out, and submerge it in a tray of cool water. Pull the strip out slowly *(left)* within 15 seconds. Lay it, paste side up, on the table and proceed with doubling over the paper as described in Step 3 *(above)*.

4 **Double the strip over from the bottom** edge in the same way *(above)*, so that the top and bottom edges almost touch. Folding the paper over itself in this way allows you to carry it without getting glue on yourself.

5 **Carry the strip over to the wall.** Unfurl the top half and press the paper into place with one edge carefully aligned against the vertical mark and an extra 2 inches extending beyond the top of the wall *(above)*.

6 **Use the brush** to smooth the paper into place and to push out any air bubbles*(above)*. Work from the top down and from the center out. Be careful that the strip remains absolutely vertical.

7 **Unfold the bottom half** and position it in place carefully along the vertical guide. Brush it down from the center towards the edges *(above)* as you did for the top half.

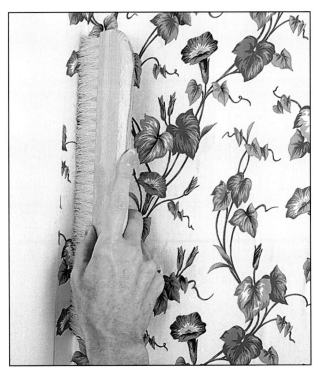

8 **In the corner,** stick the extra inch of paper to the adjacent wall. Hold the brush vertically and pound it against the paper *(above)* to push the paper into the corner. Do this also at the ceiling and baseboard.

9 **After you've pasted the strip in place,** use the putty knife to crease the paper at the ceiling corner, then use it as a straightedge and trim the excess paper with a utility knife *(above)*. Do this at the baseboard as well.

10 **Move in one direction** measuring and hanging strips. Position each one $\frac{1}{4}$ inch away from the edge of the previous strip. Glide it into place *(above)* so that the pattern matches.

11 **Butt the edges** against each other *(above)* so that they buckle slightly. As the glue dries, the paper will pull back. After 10 or 15 minutes, press the edges together with a seam roller *(inset)*, using short up-and-down strokes.

WALLPAPERING AROUND WINDOWS OR DOORS

1 **When you come to a door** or window frame, brush the strip into place as close as you can to the side of the frame *(above)* without ripping the material.

2 **Make a diagonal cut** at the top of a door frame or corners of a window frame *(above)*. Brush the top section into place, and then use the putty knife and utility knife to trim the material to fit.

3 **Follow the same procedure** down the side *(above)*. Push the covering well into place against the frame, and make sure that you make your cut where the wall meets the frame. For a window, continue along the bottom edge.

WINDOW SILLS OR MANTELS

1 **For more difficult protruding obstacles**, start by brushing the paper as close as possible from the side, taking care not to tear it. If there are tight irregular spaces, crease the paper into them with the brush or a towel.

2 Use scissors to make horizontal cuts above and below the obstacle or above and below the large protrusions *(above)*. Be careful not to make the cuts too long.

3 Use a utility knife to make finer horizontal cuts and to make any additional cuts necessary for a precise fit *(above)*. Always be sure that the covering is brushed flat against the wall and up to the protrusion.

SWITCHES OR OUTLETS

1 For switches and outlets, first turn off the electricity and remove the plate. Hang the paper directly over the fixture, then make an X-shaped slit over it *(above)*.

2 Use the putty knife as a straightedge to help cut a square of material away from the fixture slightly smaller than the plate *(above)*. Afterwards, replace the plate over the switch or outlet.

20 Hanging a Wallcovering Border

[$] Estimated Savings: $70

BEFORE YOU START

◆ To calculate how much border to buy, measure the distance to be covered and add 10 percent to account for waste resulting from matching the pattern at seams or making miter cuts. Borders are sold prepasted in 5-yard spools or, in some cases, by the yard.

◆ Choose a nondirectional pattern if the border is to be applied both horizontally and vertically. Make sure that the corners of doors, windows or other elements to be accented by the border are square; otherwise, their irregularities will be only emphasized.

◆ Prepare surfaces to ensure the border adheres well. Repair damaged spots and apply a primer-sealer. Wash painted surfaces with a mild household cleaner and rinse thoroughly. Whenever possible, remove an old wallcovering rather than apply the border over it.

◆ Complete any painting that is part of the redecorating plan. Border paste is easily wiped off painted trim and baseboards, while cleaning paint off the border will be next to impossible.

WHAT YOU NEED

Tools
- ✔ Carpenter's level
- ✔ Paintbrush
- ✔ Straightedge
- ✔ Utility knife
- ✔ Water box
- ✔ Smoothing brush
- ✔ Seam roller or sponge
- ✔ Combination square

Materials
- ✔ Plastic sheets
- ✔ Masking tape
- ✔ Primer-sealer
- ✔ Wallcovering border

1 **Plot the top edge** of the border using a carpenter's level and a pencil. Mark a bottom guideline at a distance equal to the border's width *(above)*. Don't rely on measurements taken from references such as the floor or ceiling.

2 **After taping plastic sheets** for protection along the bottom of the outline, brush on a primer-sealer *(above)*. The primer-sealer prevents paste from being absorbed into the wall and ensures good adhesion of the border.

3 **Cut the border** into manageable lengths using a utility knife and a straightedge *(above)*. Strips 4 to 6 feet in length can be handled without great difficulty and won't result in an excessive number of seams.

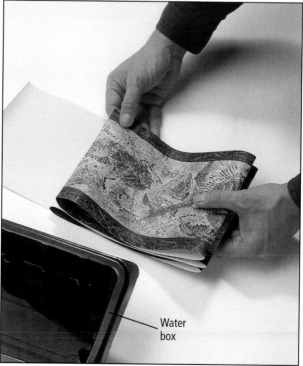

Water box

4 **Roll the strips** loosely paste-side out, then immerse them one at a time in water as specified by the manufacturer. Fold each strip paste-side to paste-side, without creasing it, into 6-inch pleats *(above)* and let it "rest" for the time specified before applying it.

VINYL-TO-VINYL ADHESIVE

If applying a border over another wallcovering, a vinyl-to-vinyl adhesive is needed to moisten the paste. After soaking each strip in water, apply the adhesive using a paste brush *(above)*.

5 **Hang the first strip** at the edge of an interruption *(above)* or in an inconspicuous corner. Align the strip to the marked guidelines; if necessary, trim the end to fit flush against the edge with a utility knife and a straightedge. To remove wrinkles and bubbles, use a smoothing brush.

6 **For a butted seam,** bring the next strip toward the preceding one *(above)* and press the ends firmly together so that they buckle slightly. As the strips dry and shrink, the buckling will disappear and the ends will flatten out.

7 **Bond the seams** after hanging four or five strips. For strong, uniform pressure, work with a seam roller. As an alternative—especially if the border is fragile and might be marred by rolling—gently press the seams together using your fingers and a damp sponge *(above)*.

MITERING CORNERS

1 **Position the second strip** so that it both overlaps and matches with the pattern of the first strip *(left)*. Unfold the strip and gently press it into place—in this case, against the edge of the wood trim around a door. Eliminate wrinkles and bubbles using a smoothing brush.

2 **Make a 45° line** from the inside corner formed by the strips to the outside edges with a combination square, setting its handle against the door trim as a guide. Draw a utility knife along the square's straightedge, pressing firmly to cut through both strips *(above)*.

3 **Peel off the top waste piece** left by the cut *(above)*. Carefully lift the trimmed edge of the overlapping strip to remove the underlying waste piece, then press the strip into place. Wait 10 to 15 minutes to roll or sponge the seam.

21 Repairing Wallcoverings
💲 Estimated Savings: $60

BEFORE YOU START

◆ Reduce humidity and improve ventilation to make a wallcovering less likely to blister, bubble, peel or lift.

◆ A permanent stain can be patched, but don't give up too quickly on trying to clean a wallcovering; lifting a persistent stain may take several attempts with different cleaners and methods.

Testing Wallcovering Resistance

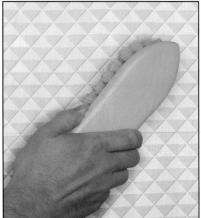

Tape a damp sponge to the wallcovering at an inconspicuous spot *(above, top)* and leave it in place for several minutes. If water doesn't penetrate the wallcovering, it is washable. If the damp spot isn't harmed by rubbing with a soft-bristled brush *(above, bottom)*, the wallcovering is scrubbable.

WHAT YOU NEED

Tools
- ✔ Utility knife or artist's knife
- ✔ Syringe-type glue injector
- ✔ Straightedge
- ✔ Artist's brush
- ✔ Small paste brush
- ✔ Sponge
- ✔ Seam roller
- ✔ Putty knife

Materials
- ✔ Wallcovering
- ✔ Wallcovering paste

BLISTERS

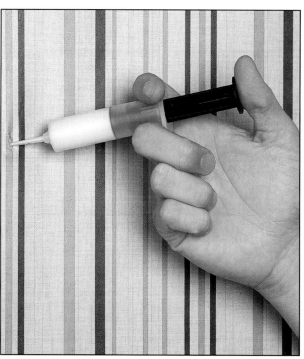

1 **Pierce the blister** with the point of a sharp blade, cutting a slit that is just large enough to fit in the tip of a glue injector *(above)*.

2 **Insert the tip** of a glue injector into the slit and squirt out a small amount of paste *(above)*. Then, press against the surface and wipe off excess adhesive with a damp sponge.

BUBBLES

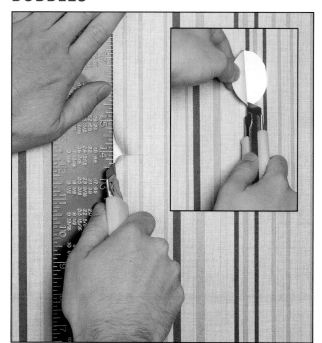

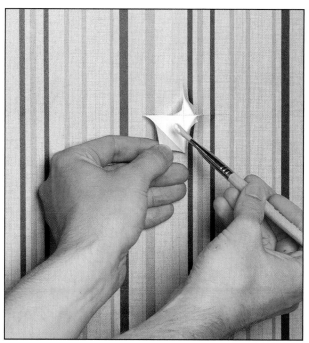

1 **Moisten the bubble** with a damp sponge, then open it by making two crosswise passes with a utility knife and a straightedge *(above)*. Alternatively, cut a semicircle around the edge of the bubble *(inset)*.

2 **Carefully apply paste** to the back of each flap and to the wall with an artist's brush *(above)*. Press the flaps into place and wipe off excess adhesive with a damp sponge.

PEELING OR LIFTING

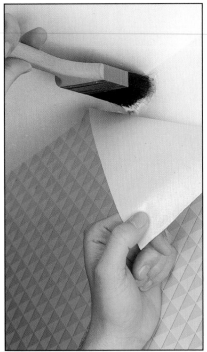 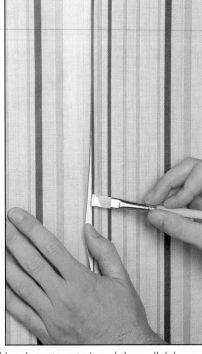 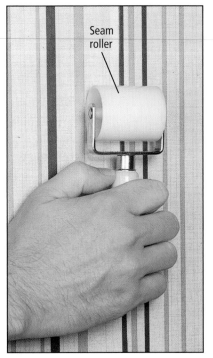

1 **Gently pull back** a peeling edge and brush paste onto it and the wall *(above, left)*. Raise a lifted edge just enough to apply paste with an artist's paintbrush *(above, right)*. Let the paste stand for about 5 minutes.

2 **Press the edge** into place and smooth it *(above)*. Wipe off excess adhesive with a damp sponge.

APPLIQUÉ OVERLAY PATCH

Artist's knife

1 **Prepare a patch** for a large, distinctive shape in a pattern using a matching scrap of wallcovering, cutting out the identical shape with a sharp blade *(above)*.

2 **Brush water** onto the patch if it is prepasted; otherwise, apply paste. Position the patch *(above)*, then smooth it and wipe off excess paste with a damp sponge.

TORN OVERLAY PATCH

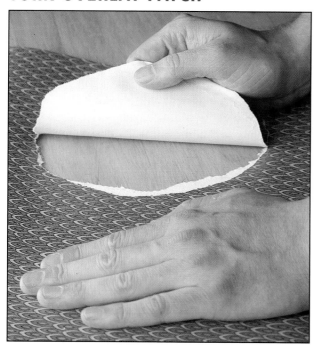 

1 Tear a patch of matching wallcovering for small, busy patterns, pulling upward and twisting slightly to feather the underside edges *(above)*. (Practice the technique on scraps of the same or similar material.)

2 Dip the patch in water if it is prepasted; otherwise brush on paste. Position the patch so that its pattern matches the surface and press it into place *(above)*. Smooth the patch and wipe off excess paste with a damp sponge.

DOUBLE-CUT PATCH

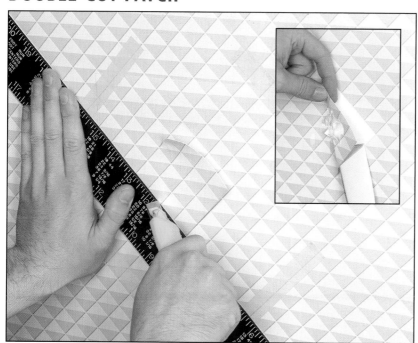 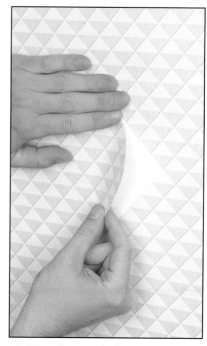

1 Tape a matching piece in place, carefully aligning the pattern. With a utility knife and a straightedge, cut a patch and slice through the underlying layer *(above, left)*; if possible, cut along pattern lines. Remove the patch and the piece it was cut from, then peel off the underlying layer *(above, right)*.

2 Wet the patch if it is prepasted; otherwise, apply paste. Press the patch into place *(above)*, then wipe off excess paste with a damp sponge.

71

22 Regrouting Rigid Tiles
💲 Estimated Savings: $30 per sq. ft.

BEFORE YOU START

◆ Purchase grout containing sand to fill joints $\frac{1}{8}$ inch or more in width. For narrower joints, buy unsanded grout.

◆ Grout made with Portland cement is inconspicuous and doesn't show dirt; as well, it can be tinted with powdered coloring. Precise color-matching of the original grout can be difficult—and will likely take a number of test batches.

◆ When preparing grout, mix together the dry ingredients and slowly add in the liquid ingredients until the grout is spreadable without being runny.

◆ Plan to wait at least 12 hours for regrouted joints to harden before subjecting them to foot traffic. If a sealer of liquid silicone is to be applied to the joints, allow the grout to cure for a minimum of 7 days.

WHAT YOU NEED

Tools
- ✔ Grout saw
- ✔ Whisk broom
- ✔ Mixing container
- ✔ Grout float
- ✔ Pail
- ✔ Old toothbrush

Materials
- ✔ Grout
- ✔ Cloths
- ✔ Sponge

SAFETY FIRST

Wear safety goggles and a dust mask when scraping old grout out of joints. Wear rubber gloves to avoid skin contact with grout.

1 **Scrape old grout** out of the joints with a grout saw *(above)*. Sweep away particles and dust, then dampen the cleaned joints with water.

2 **Prepare enough grout** for the job. With a grout float, spread grout across the tiles and force it into the joints *(above)*. Alternatively, pack grout into one joint at a time with a finger *(inset)*.

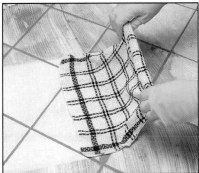

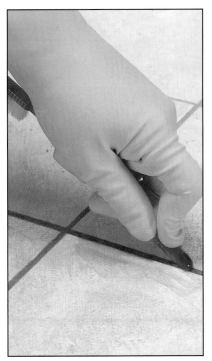

3 **Clear excess grout** off the tiles *(above, top)* and allow the joints to harden for 2 or 3 minutes. Then, wipe the tiles clean by dragging a wet cloth across them *(above, bottom)*.

4 **Wait 15 minutes** if the tiles are beveled at the edges. Then, run along each joint with the end of an old toothbrush, smoothing and shaping the grout *(above)*.

5 **Wipe the tiles** clean with a damp sponge *(above)*. Let the flooring dry, then wash off the hazy film remaining. Wait 12 hours, then rub stray grout off the tiles with a nonmetallic scouring pad.

23 Replacing a Laminate Countertop
$ Estimated Savings: $105

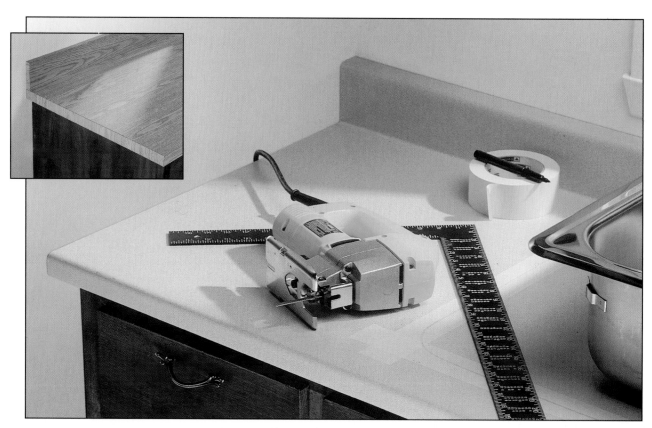

BEFORE YOU START

Laminated countertop is available in a wide variety of colors and patterns in two different styles:

◆ Postform, which features a continuous work surface and backsplash with a gently curving joint and rounded face edge *(above)*.

◆ Custom self-edge, with backsplash and face edge at a 90° angle to the work surface *(inset)*.

Measuring for Countertop

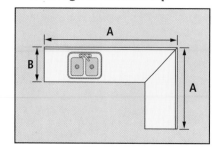

Precise measurements of the existing countertop will ensure that installation of its replacement goes smoothly:

◆ **A** Measure the length of each section along the backsplash.

◆ **B** Check the width; if it differs from the standard 25 inches, specify the measurement when ordering.

WHAT YOU NEED

Tools
- ✔ Open-end wrenches
- ✔ Basin wrench
- ✔ Screwdriver
- ✔ Utility knife
- ✔ Electric drill
- ✔ Caulking gun
- ✔ Saber saw

Materials
- ✔ Laminated countertop
- ✔ Kraft paper
- ✔ Masking tape
- ✔ Corner fasteners
- ✔ Screws
- ✔ Silicone caulk

SAFETY FIRST

Shut off electricity to the garbage disposer and dishwasher. Turn off the water supply to the sink and open the faucet to drain the supply tubes. Wear safety goggles when using an electric drill and a saber saw.

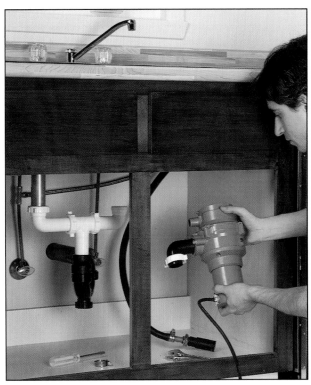

1 **Disconnect drain fittings** and dishwasher plumbing, then dismount the garbage disposer *(above)*. Remove the supply tubes from the faucet with a basin wrench.

2 **Unscrew the anchors** below the countertop that secure the sink *(inset)*. Separate the sink from the countertop with a utility knife, then lift it out *(above)*.

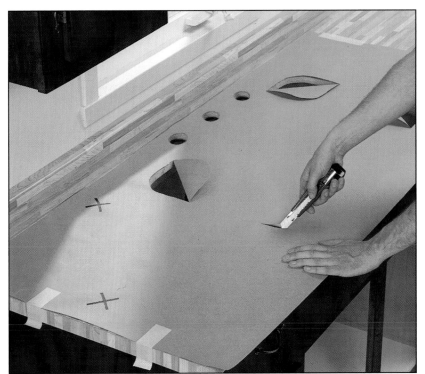

3 **Tape a paper template** across the sink cutout flush against the backsplash and even with one end of the countertop; mark each reference edge with an X, as shown. With a utility knife, cut through the template to make an opening at any holes for the faucet and at each corner of the sink cutout *(above)*.

4 **Remove the screws** that hold the countertop to the dishwasher *(above)* and interior corners of the cabinets, then lift off the countertop.

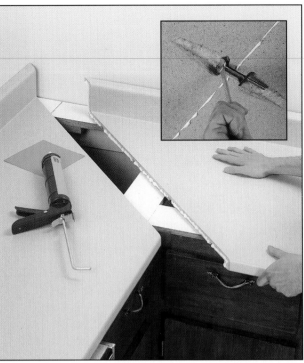

5 **Slide the new countertop** into place on the cabinets *(above, left)*. To join two sections of an L-shaped countertop, apply a bead of caulk along one of the mitered edges and press the sections together *(above, right)*. Insert corner fasteners into the precut channels underneath the countertop at the joint, then tighten them in turn from back to front with a wrench *(inset)*. Wipe off excess caulk.

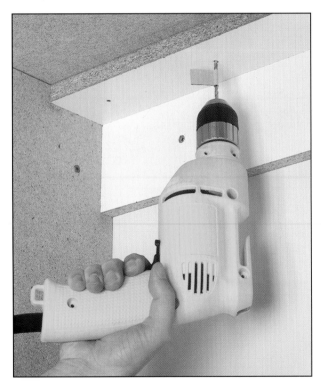

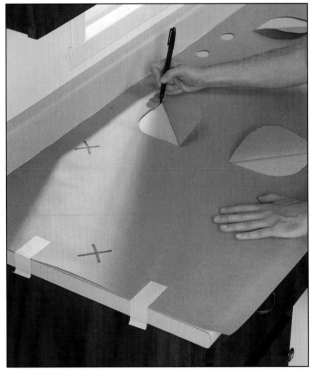

6 **Bore pilot holes** for screws through existing holes in the cabinet supports, using masking tape wrapped around the bit as a depth guide *(above)*. Screw the countertop in place and secure the dishwasher to it.

7 **Tape the template** to the countertop, using the reference marks to align it correctly. Transfer the corners of the sink cutout onto the countertop *(above)*, then remove the template and draw straight lines between the corners.

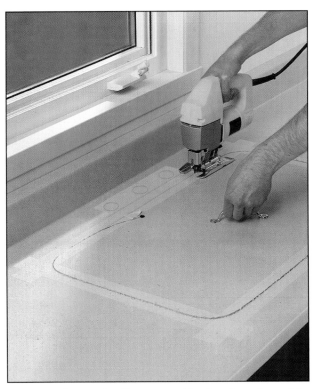

8 **Tape the cutting lines** to avoid splintering edges while sawing—darken them enough to be visible. Fasten a handle to the waste piece of the sink cutout for support, then drill a blade entry hole and cut with a saber saw *(above)*.

9 **Set the sink** in the cutout and adjust it until the drain aligns with the drainpipe, then draw reference lines from adjacent edges onto the countertop *(above)*. Remove the sink and apply a bead of caulk along the edges of the cutout, then reposition it using the reference lines.

10 **Reconnect the supply tubes** to the faucet, then mount the garbage disposer, attach dishwasher plumbing and reconnect drain fittings *(above)*. Screw in the anchors that hold the sink in place.

11 **Fill the gap** between the backsplash and the wall with a bead of caulk *(above)*. Smooth the caulk with a wet finger and wipe off excess.

24 Refacing Cabinets

$ Estimated Savings: $240

WHAT YOU NEED

Tools
- ✔ Circular saw
- ✔ Small paint roller
- ✔ Claw hammer
- ✔ Sanding block
- ✔ Utility knife
- ✔ Combination square
- ✔ Hand roller
- ✔ Screwdriver
- ✔ Fine-toothed handsaw
- ✔ Backsaw and miter box
- ✔ Electric drill
- ✔ Awl
- ✔ Carpenter's level

Materials
- ✔ Lauan plywood
- ✔ Contact cement
- ✔ Brads
- ✔ Paper or plastic sheeting
- ✔ Masking tape
- ✔ Clear lacquer spray
- ✔ Medium sandpaper
- ✔ Veneer
- ✔ Trim molding
- ✔ Finishing nails
- ✔ Finish touch-up kit
- ✔ Drawer fronts
- ✔ Doors
- ✔ Hinges
- ✔ Knobs, pulls or handles

BEFORE YOU START

◆ Order drawer fronts, drawers and veneer through a refacing specialist or cabinetmaker. For the face frames, ask for peel-and-stick veneer; obtain sheet veneer for the end panels. Also request matching prefinished trim molding and a finish touch-up kit.

◆ Strip painted end panels and face frames. Fill holes with wood filler and sand surfaces smooth. Prepare surfaces

for veneer by spraying them with three coats of clear lacquer.

◆ Save old pieces of trim molding as guides for cutting new pieces. Use the holes in old drawer fronts and doors as reference when installing knobs, pulls or handles on the replacements.

◆ Mount plastic or felt bumpers on the inside of new drawer fronts and doors to protect the veneer.

SAFETY FIRST

Wear safety goggles and a dust mask when sawing wood. Ventilate the work area to apply lacquer and contact cement.

END PANELS

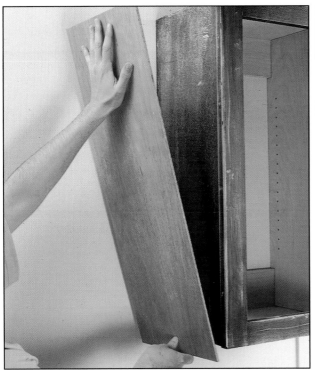

1 **Cut plywood** to fit the cabinet end and bring it flush with the edge of the face frame. Coat the plywood and cabinet end with contact cement, then press the plywood into place *(above, left)* and secure it with brads. Tape paper over adjacent surfaces to protect them, then apply three coats of lacquer to the plywood *(above, right)*.

2 **Trace the cabinet end** onto the back of sheet veneer *(above)*. Trim the veneer $\frac{1}{16}$ inch larger than the marked outline with a circular saw.

3 **Coat the veneer** and cabinet end with contact cement. Aligning the veneer with the inner edge and top of the cabinet, press it into place *(above)*.

4 **Sand protruding edges** of the veneer flush with the bottom and outer edge of the cabinet *(above)*. Reapply lacquer to surfaces sanded.

STILES AND RAILS

Stile

Rail

1 **For each end stile,** cut a veneer strip $\frac{1}{2}$ inch wider and longer. Peel the backing off the strip and press the veneer into place *(above)*.

2 **Trim the veneer** flush with the edges of the end stile using a utility knife *(above)*, but leave the overlap on each rail.

3 **For top and bottom rails,** apply and trim veneer so that it overlaps the stiles. At each end, slice through the overlap *(above)* and remove the waste pieces to make a butt joint.

4 **Veneer intermediate stiles** next, slicing through overlap and removing the waste pieces to make butt joints at the top and bottom rails. Then, veneer the intermediate rails *(above)* and cut butt joints at the stiles.

5 **Run a hand roller** along the stiles and rails *(above)* to bond the veneer. Nail trim molding along gaps with the walls, ceiling or floor.

DRAWER FRONTS

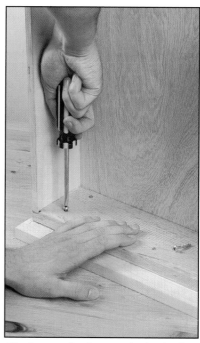

1 Unscrew the old front from the box, if possible. Otherwise, remove the glides and trim the front flush with the box *(above)*, then screw the glides back on in line with the trimmed front *(inset)*. At each corner of the front, bore a screw clearance hole.

2 Center the box on the back of the new front and mark the hole locations. Bore pilot holes, then screw through the box into the front *(above)*.

DOORS

1 Screw hinges to doors at the same distance from the top and bottom. Center each door on its opening and check that it sits square with a carpenter's level, then mark screw locations *(above)*, bore pilot holes and screw on the hinges.

2 Align subsequent doors using the mounted ones as reference *(above)*. Leave a gap of $\frac{1}{8}$ inch between doors being mounted on the same opening.

25 Installing Molding & Chair Rails
$ Estimated Savings: $250

BEFORE YOU START

◆ Installing a chair rail will change the character of a room dramatically. A traditional treatment *(left)* includes a $2\frac{1}{2}$-inch Colonial contoured casing for the rail, topped with a strip of $1\frac{1}{4}$-inch pine "bullnose" molding painted to match the wall color and coordinated with the wallpaper above the rail.

◆ A chart on page 84 shows a variety of combinations of moldings and casings that can be mounted as chair rails. These materials are commonly available where wood products are sold. Contoured moldings are harder to fit and join at the corners than a plain, flat length of lumber. The casing and molding shown in the instructions are WM 366 and WM 250 respectively.

◆ For a traditional look, paper the wall above the rail. Paint the wall below the rail (also called a "dado") to coordinate with the wallpaper. More elegantly, add decorative panels of wood wainscoting below the railing.

◆ For a more contemporary style, paint the chair rail the same light tone as the wall. An interesting variation is to leave the molding natural and wax or varnish it if that would not create a distracting stripe around the room.

◆ If the chair rail is interrupted by a window at any point in the room, make sure the height of the rail is the same as the window's sill, or higher. If it passes below the window it will look out of place.

WHAT YOU NEED

Tools
- ✔ Tape measure
- ✔ Chalk line
- ✔ Backsaw and miter box
- ✔ Coping saw
- ✔ Hammer
- ✔ Electric drill
- ✔ Nail set

Materials
- ✔ Plain or contoured casing
- ✔ Top molding
- ✔ 6d finishing nails (casing)
- ✔ 8d finishing nails (molding)
- ✔ Wood filler
- ✔ Sandpaper
- ✔ Primer and paint or other finish

SAFETY FIRST

Sand any rough edges before starting work. You may want to wear gloves to avoid splinters along edges of rails or moldings.

MEASURING, CUTTING AND ATTACHING CASINGS

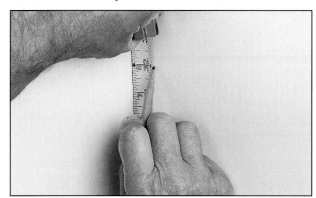

1 At one end of the wall measure up from the floor to where you want the top of the casing to be (35 inches is common). Mark that spot on the wall in one corner *(above)*. Repeat at the other end of that wall. The molding will be set on top of the casing later, adding its height to the finished rail.

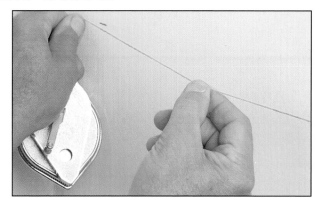

2 Drive a nail partway into the stud at one mark. Attach a chalk line to it and hold the other end at the other corner mark. Pull the line taut. Lift it about 1 inch away from the wall *(above)* and let it snap gently to make a level line for positioning the casing.

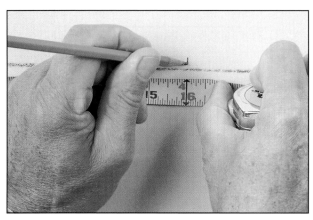

3 Mark the location of each stud along the wall. Tap until you hear a solid sound—usually 16 inches apart. Before nailing, test each location by driving a nail partway into the wall at the chalk line. The molding will cover the marks and holes.

4 Measure from corner to corner along one wall. Be sure both ends will reach *all* the way into the corners. Cut the length of casing with the ends square *(above)*. The casing on the adjoining wall will butt to it.

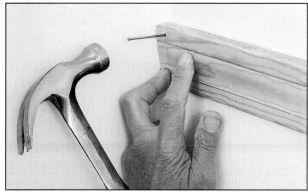

5 Have a helper hold one end of the casing on the chalk line or prop it there. Nail the other end into the corner stud with two 6d "brights" finishing nails. Set the nail heads slightly below the surface.

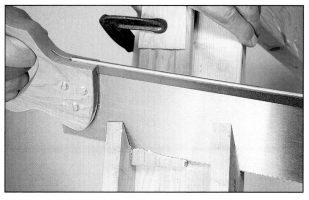

6 Repeat steps #1-5 on adjoining walls, again measuring the full length corner-to-corner. Cut the ends at a 45° bevel into the molded face of the casing. Clamp the casing in a miter box and cut the bevel with a backsaw *(above)*.

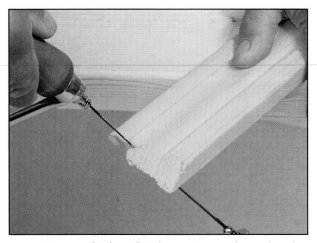

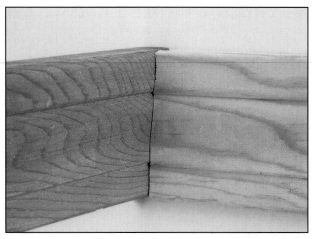

7 **Cut away the bevel** with a coping saw by angling the blade so it cuts away from the bevel into the back and exactly follows the line of the contour on the front *(above)*. This creates a sharp-edged contour to fit the other casing.

8 **Fit the newly cut edge** in place. Make any minor adjustments to the coped contour with a razor knife, sandpaper, or coping saw. Nail either end of the casing into the corner stud with 6d finishing nails. Set the nail heads.

SOME POPULAR COMBINATIONS OF CASINGS AND MOLDINGS FOR CHAIR RAILS

The illustrations below show, in cross-sectional view, the shapes of some one-piece chair rails and combinations of casings and moldings that can be mounted together as chair rails. The code numbers below each one are used by most vendors to identify those specific shapes.

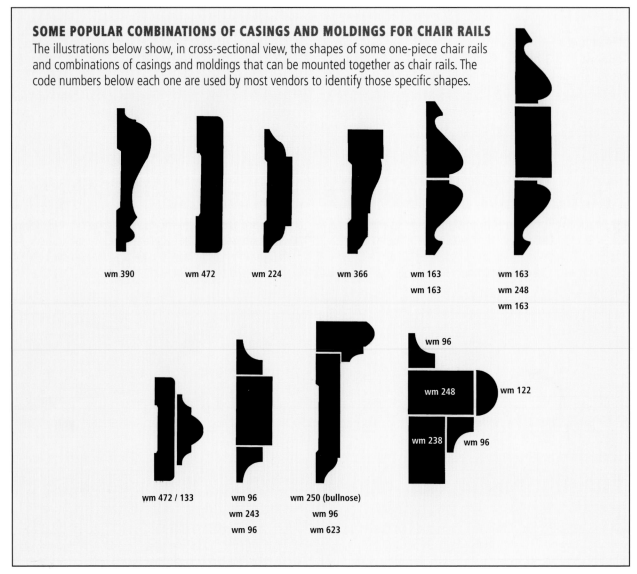

wm 390

wm 472

wm 224

wm 366

wm 163
wm 163

wm 163
wm 248
wm 163

wm 96

wm 248

wm 122

wm 238

wm 96

wm 472 / 133

wm 96
wm 243
wm 96

wm 250 (bullnose)
wm 96
wm 623

MEASURING, CUTTING AND ATTACHING NOSE MOLDING

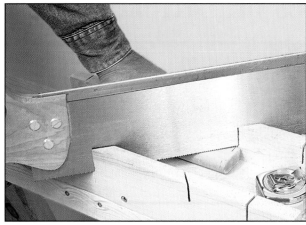

1 Measure the length to cut the bullnose molding (WM 250 on page 84) from corner to corner along the top of each casing. Cut the ends of each length at a 45° angle with a backsaw and miter box *(above)*, not squared off.

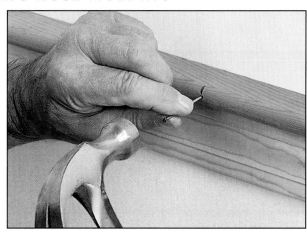

2 Nail one length along the top of its casing at each stud with 8d "brights" *(above)*. Mark the spots lined up with the two nails in the casing below. To minimize the risk of splitting, predrill the nail holes.

3 Hold the end of the adjoining molding in place at the corner to check that the two mitered ends fit together perfectly *(above)*. Adjust a cut, if necessary, before gently nailing the end of the loose molding into place.

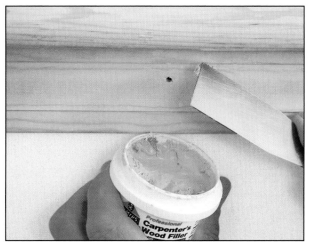

4 Fill nail holes and any cracks in mitered and coped cuts with wood filler *(above)*. Smooth it with a finger. When dry, sand seams and surfaces lightly. Apply the finish after installation to cover scuffs and pencil marks.

WHERE CASING AND MOLDING MEET OTHER TRIM

Where a casing meets the trim of a door, window or fireplace, cut the butting end square at 90°. Where the nose molding meets the trim, one option is to round the end and cut a notch out of its back so it overlaps the trim *(right)*.

26 Hanging Frames on Different Walls

$ Estimated Savings: $35

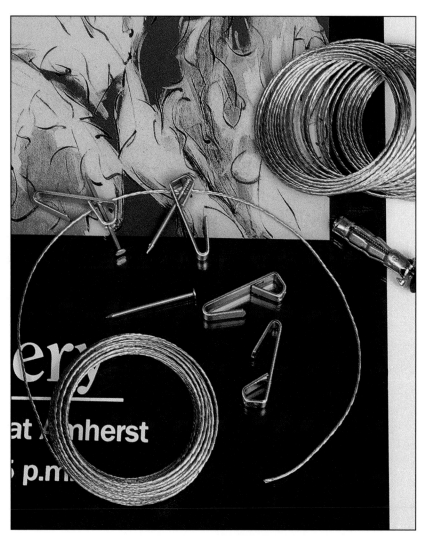

BEFORE YOU START

◆ If hanging a picture or mirror on a hollow wall (drywall or plaster), check for a stud (a wooden 2-by-4 behind the wall) where you plan to hang your picture. Studs are usually spaced 16 or 24 inches apart; with drywall, you can sometimes see a seam where two panels meet, and the center of the stud will be behind the seam. Alternatively, you can use a stud finder (page 192) or tap on the wall and listen for a dull thud rather than a hollow sound. Use wall anchors to hang between studs. The box of anchors lists how much weight they will hold and what size drill bit to use.

WALL ANCHORS

A wall anchor holds a weight-bearing screw or bolt securely in place in wall material where a nail or anchorless screw would slip out too easily: hollow drywall, plaster, thin plywood, or masonry (including the mortar between bricks). Modern anchors are self-drilling (opposite page) but older types (above) require that you first drill a hole through the wallboard, tap the anchor through with a hammer and expand it by turning the bolt on its face.

WHAT YOU NEED

IF YOU CAN LOCATE A STUD IN THE RIGHT LOCATION:	IF YOU CANNOT LOCATE A STUD IN THE RIGHT LOCATION:
Tools	**Tools**
✔ Hammer	✔ Phillips screwdriver
Materials	✔ Electric drill (for traditional anchor-types only)
✔ Picture hook with matching nail	**Materials**
	✔ Wall anchor with matching screw
	✔ Washer

HANGING A PICTURE OR MIRROR ON A HOLLOW WALL

1 **Hold up the picture** to where you want it to hang, and lightly mark the center of the top edge with a pencil *(above)*. (To be sure you have the picture in the right location, it helps to have an assistant hold it while you look at it from a distance.)

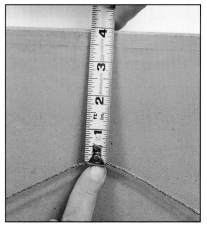

2 **Pull up** on the picture's hanging wire with your finger, and measure the distance between the wire and the top edge of the picture *(above)*. Measure that same distance down from your mark on the wall, and draw a small X with the pencil where the picture will hang.

FOR LIGHT PICTURES OR NAILING INTO STUDS

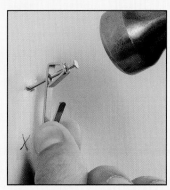

Use a picture hook for very light frames or if you can nail into wood or a stud. Place a small piece of cellophane tape on the wall to reduce damage to surface finish.

3 **If there is no stud** in the right spot, drill a hole the diameter recommended on the package for the anchor you're using. Insert the anchor, or drive a self-drilling anchor into the X *(above, left)*. Place a washer onto the screw and drive it into place *(above, right)*. The washer prevents the hanging wire from slipping off the screw. Hangers that slip over the screw are also available.

HANGING A FULL-LENGTH MIRROR

To mount a light mirror suitable for bedroom or bathroom, use clear plastic holders that mount at the edge of the mirror and screw directly into the wall. To mount on a hollow wall, fasten the top and bottom holders into studs behind the wall.

FOR CEMENT OR BRICK

Lead anchors are used in masonry walls (as well as in the mortar between bricks) to secure loads of any weight. After drilling a hole with a masonry drill bit or hand-held "star" drill, insert the anchor and then drive a screw into the hollow center of the anchor, which will then expand to lock firmly against the sides of the hole. Masonry anchors may also be made of plastic or fiber.

27 Correcting Interior Doors
💲 Estimated Savings: $60

BEFORE YOU START

Observe the following sequence when planning repairs to an interior door that doesn't open and close as it should:

◆ **Hardware:** Make adjustments to the hinges and strike plate.
◆ **Door:** Sand, plane or trim edges.
◆ **Frame:** Reposition the stop or shim out or draw in the jambs.

Binding Remedies

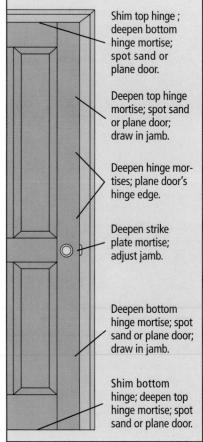

Shim top hinge ; deepen bottom hinge mortise; spot sand or plane door.

Deepen top hinge mortise; spot sand or plane door; draw in jamb.

Deepen hinge mortises; plane door's hinge edge.

Deepen strike plate mortise; adjust jamb.

Deepen bottom hinge mortise; spot sand or plane door; draw in jamb.

Shim bottom hinge; deepen top hinge mortise; spot sand or plane door.

WHAT YOU NEED

HARDWARE	DOOR	FRAME
Tools	**Tools**	**Tools**
✔ Screwdriver	✔ Sanding block	✔ Utility bar
✔ Claw hammer	✔ Nail set	✔ Putty knife
✔ Utility knife	✔ Claw hammer	✔ Claw hammer
✔ Wood chisel	✔ Screwdrivers	✔ Bench plane
✔ File	✔ Mallet	✔ Hacksaw
✔ Paring gouge	✔ Bench plane	✔ Locking pliers
✔ Mallet	✔ Block plane	✔ Screwdriver
Materials	✔ Circular saw	**Materials**
✔ Dowels	**Materials**	✔ Shims
✔ Wood glue	✔ Sandpaper	✔ Finishing nails
✔ Cardboard		✔ Wood screws

SAFETY FIRST

Wear safety goggles and a dust mask to use a circular saw.

HARDWARE ADJUSTMENTS

Tightening hinges. Cut dowels to fit the screw holes, then coat them with glue and tap them into place *(above)*. Wait at least an hour, then bore pilot holes and screw in the hinge.

Shimming hinges. Cut a cardboard shim the same size as the hinge and insert it into the mortise *(above)*, then drive in the screws. (If necessary, add a second shim.)

Deepening hinge mortises. Cut the mortise to the required depth with a wood chisel, holding it bevel down and applying only hand pressure *(above)*. Then, reseat and screw in the hinge.

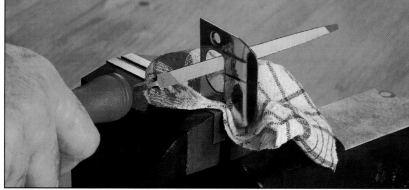

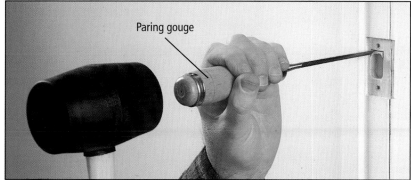

Paring gouge

Relocating strike plates. Rub the edge of the latch bolt with crayon and close the door, then open it and mark the position to which the strike plate must be shifted *(above, left)*. If the distance is less than $\frac{1}{8}$ inch, unscrew the strike plate and enlarge its opening with a file *(above right, top)*. Otherwise, extend the mortise and enlarge the bolt hole with a wood chisel and a paring gouge *(above right, bottom)*.

DOOR MODIFICATIONS

Spot sanding. Sand rubbing spots on the door with medium sandpaper on a sanding block *(above)*. (To reach top, bottom and hinged edges, the door may need to be removed.)

REMOVING DOORS

 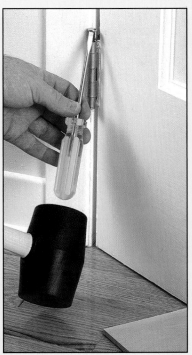

With the door propped open on a shim, take the pin out of the bottom hinge and then the top hinge. Raise each pin with a nail set and a hammer *(above, left)*, then tap it out using an old screwdriver and a mallet *(above, right)*.

Planing sides. To support the door, make two jacks out of scrap plywood *(inset)*. Unscrew the hinges from the door, then trim the side edge with a bench plane *(left)*. (If $\frac{1}{8}$ inch or more is cut off the edge, deepen the hinge mortises.)

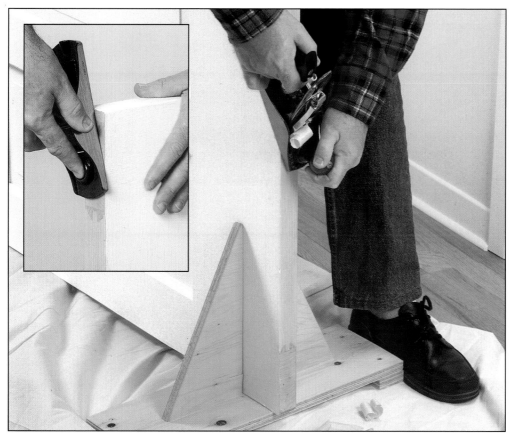

Planing tops and bottoms. With the door supported at each end in a jack, trim the length of the edge using a bench plane *(left)*. For end grain, trim with a block plane *(inset)*.

Sawing bottoms. To cut $\frac{1}{4}$ inch or more off the bottom edge, support the door securely on a pair of sawhorses. Mark a cutting line on the door and clamp a straight board in place as a saw guide, then make the cut with a circular saw *(left)*.

WARPED DOOR

For a door that is warped across its width, add a third hinge at the center to hold it straight *(inset)*. To straighten a door that is warped along its height, clamp shims at the center of the high points *(right)* and tighten the clamps periodically over a few days.

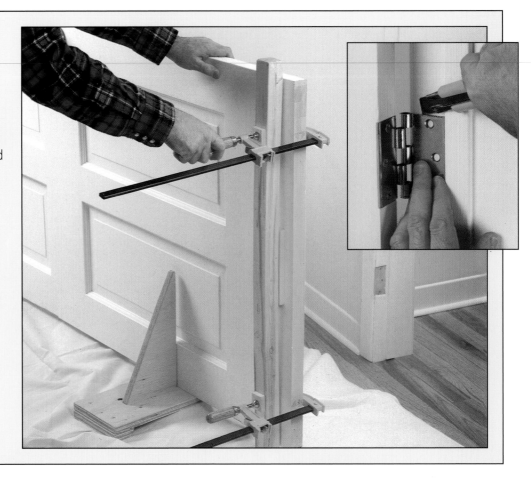

FRAME ADJUSTMENTS

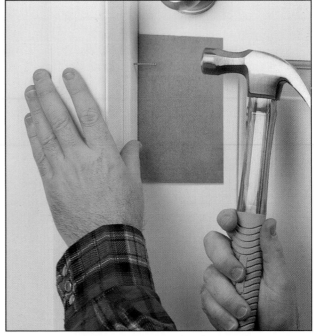

Repositioning stops. Pry off the stop with a utility bar, protecting the jamb with a putty knife *(above, left)*. With the door closed, reposition the stop and nail it into place using a thin piece of cardboard as a spacer *(above, right)*.

REMOVING TRIM

To shim out or draw in a jamb, the stop and the trim around the door frame need to be removed. Raise the trim with a utility bar, using a putty knife to protect the wall. To avoid damaging the trim, slip the blade of a hacksaw behind it and cut the nails *(above)*.

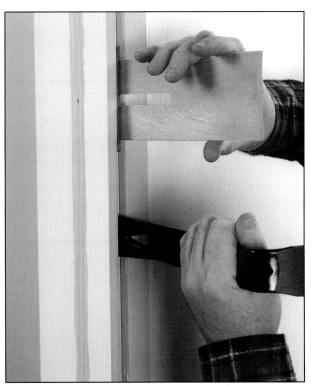

Shimming out jambs. Cut a $\frac{1}{2}$-inch notch in a shim with a utility knife, then pry the jamb out far enough to insert it between the other shims and around the nail securing them *(above)*. Drive a 4-inch finishing nail through the jamb to hold the shim in place and trim off the protruding end.

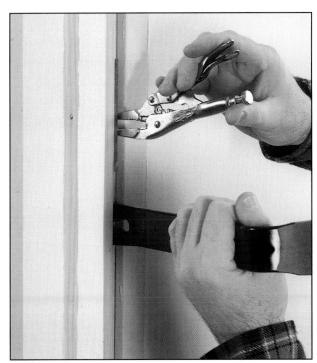

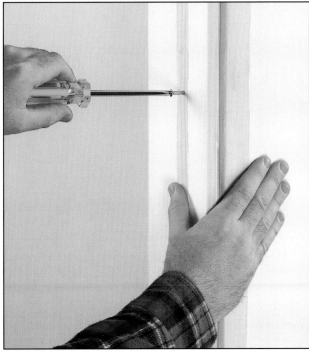

Drawing in jambs. Pry the jamb out far enough to fit locking pliers around the nail securing the shims *(above, left)*, then press against it to raise the nail head. Pull the nail out slowly with the pliers until a shim falls loose, then drive it back in. Drive a 3-inch wood screw into the jamb at the center of the high point *(above, right)*.

28 Framing an Interior Wall
💲 Estimated Savings: $120

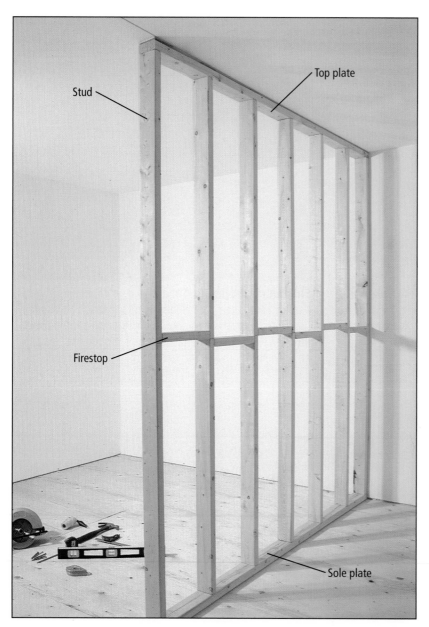

Stud

Top plate

Firestop

Sole plate

BEFORE YOU START
◆ Clear a workspace large enough to assemble the frame flat on the floor.
◆ Select the straightest 2-by-4s available for the sole and top plates and the end studs; a slight warp in other boards is acceptable.
◆ Locate hidden ceiling joists and wall studs with a stud finder.

Adding Nailing Blocks

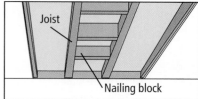

Joist

Nailing block

When a wall frame is put up parallel to joists, it must be secured to nailing blocks of the same stock as the joists—unless it is positioned directly under one joist. Space the blocks no more than 24 inches apart *(above)*.

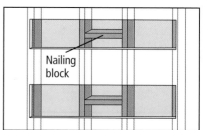

Nailing block

To anchor a wall frame that meets an existing wall between studs, cut a pair of 2-by-4 nailing blocks. Fasten one block about $2\frac{1}{2}$ feet from the bottom of the wall and the other the same distance from the top *(above)*.

SAFETY FIRST

Wear safety goggles when using a circular saw and driving nails. Wear a dust mask to cut lumber.

WHAT YOU NEED

Tools		Materials
✔ Chalk line	✔ Combination square	✔ 2-by-4s
✔ Stepladder	✔ Circular saw	✔ Common nails
✔ Plumb bob	✔ Claw hammer	($3\frac{1}{2}$-inch)
✔ Tape measure	✔ Carpenter's level	✔ Wood shims
	✔ Utility knife	

1 **Mark the wall location** on the floor with a chalk line *(above)*. Using a plumb bob to transfer the endpoints of the line, snap the wall position on the ceiling *(right)* or across the joists or nailing blocks. Mark joist locations on the ceiling.

2 **Cut 2-by-4s to length** for the sole and top plates. Mark one end of each plate for reference, then mark off the centers of studs. Outline the locations of studs on the plates with a combination square *(above)*.

3 **Subtract 3 inches** from the shortest distance between the floor and ceiling at the wall location, then cut studs to this length using a circular saw *(above)*.

4 **To assemble the frame,** position the studs between the sole and top plates at the marked locations. Then, drive two nails into each end of the studs through the plates *(above)*.

5 **Raise the frame** into place *(above, left)* and align the sole and top plates with the chalked lines. Hold a carpenter's level against the studs at several points to make sure that the frame is plumb, then shim the top plate *(above, right)* to secure it.

6 **Nail the sole plate** to the floor *(above, left)* every 16 inches—if possible, to joists. (If the floor is concrete, use 2½-inch hardened concrete nails.) Fasten the top plate to the ceiling joists *(above, right)* or nailing blocks, then trim the shims with a utility knife. To tie the frame to an existing wall, nail the end stud to a stud or nailing blocks.

7 **Cut 2-by-4 firestops** to fit between the studs, then nail them into place at alternating levels about halfway between the sole and top plates *(above).*

FRAMING A CORNER

When building a corner, add a stud and two 2-by-4 nailing blocks to brace it and provide fastening surfaces for drywall. Nail the blocks to the end stud at about one-third and two-thirds of its height, then fasten the reinforcing stud to the blocks and to the sole and top plates.

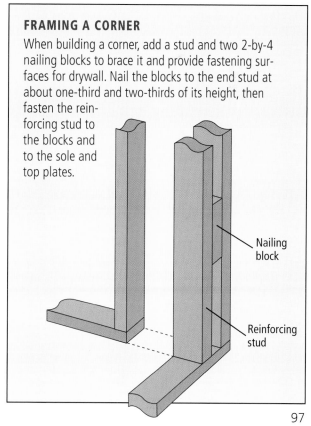

Nailing block

Reinforcing stud

29 Hanging Drywall
💲 Estimated Savings: $55 per 100 sq. ft.

BEFORE YOU START

◆ Complete electrical wiring and other utility installations. Check that exterior walls are adequately insulated.

◆ To determine the number of drywall panels to buy, divide the square footage (including all but large openings) by the area of a panel—32 square feet for a standard 4- by 8-foot panel.

◆ Plan to install panels on the ceiling first, then the walls—always beginning at a corner. Measure and cut panels so that end-to-end joints fall at joists or studs and are staggered by at least 16 inches in adjacent rows. Except on short runs of wall, hang panels horizontally to reduce the number of joints.

ADDING CEILING NAILING BLOCKS

If an end joist lies more than 4 inches from a wall, add L-shaped 2-by-4 nailing blocks every 24 inches or so to provide fastening surfaces for panels *(below)*.

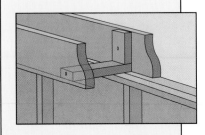

WHAT YOU NEED

Tools
- ✔ Caulking gun
- ✔ Electric drill with clutch driver
- ✔ Tape measure
- ✔ Utility knife
- ✔ Drywall saws
- ✔ Drywall T-square
- ✔ Claw hammer
- ✔ Putty knives: 5-inch and 8-inch
- ✔ Drywall knife: 10-inch
- ✔ Corner trowel
- ✔ Sanding plate and extension pole
- ✔ Sanding block
- ✔ Drywall sponge

Materials
- ✔ Drywall panels
- ✔ Drywall adhesive
- ✔ Drywall screws
- ✔ Corner bead
- ✔ Drywall nails
- ✔ Joint compound
- ✔ Joint tape
- ✔ Fine sandpaper

✋ SAFETY FIRST

Wear safety goggles to drive fasteners and apply joint compound directly overhead. Wear a dust mask when sanding joint compound.

PUTTING UP CEILING PANELS

1 **Mark the center** of each joist and nailing block on the top plate of the wall *(above)*. (These fastening surfaces will be hidden when drywall panels are positioned.)

2 **With a caulking gun,** lay a bead of adhesive along each joist and nailing block fastening surface *(above)*.

T-brace

3 **Supporting a drywall panel** in position with a T-brace, fasten it to the joists at 12-inch intervals with 1½-inch screws *(above)*. Drive each screw just far enough into the drywall to dimple the surface *(inset)*.

MEASUREMENT TRANSFERS

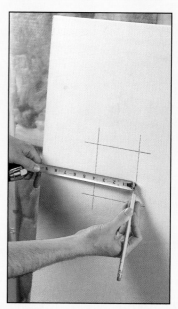

Hold a tape measure opened at the distance being transferred against the edge of the panel and place a pencil at the end of the tape, then move both hands at the same time steadily down the panel to mark it *(above)*.

With a utility knife and a straightedge, score the outline of the opening and cut an X from corner to corner across it. Prop the panel on wood blocks, then punch out the cutout *(above)*.

4 **Make openings** for electrical boxes with a small dry-wall saw *(above)*, punching the tip of the blade through the panel to start cutting.

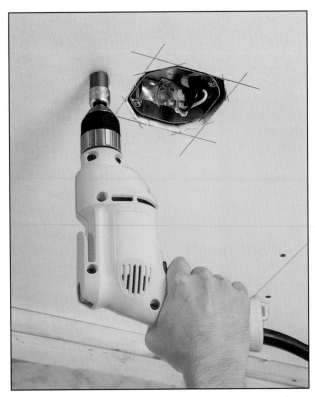

5 **Test-fit panels** and adjust openings as necessary, then secure them in place with adhesive and screws *(above)*.

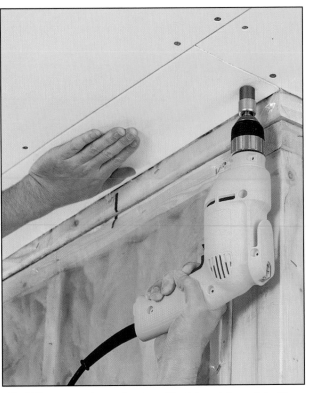

6 **Fill gaps** at the perimeter with strips of drywall, butting them against the length of adjacent panels so that the tapered edges meet *(above)*.

SCORE, SNAP, CUT

For cuts straight across panels, score a cutting line with a utility knife and a drywall T-square *(above, left)*. Snap a clean break in the panel along the scored line *(above, center)*, then cut through the back paper *(above, right)*.

MOUNTING WALL PANELS

1 Mark stud locations on the ceiling and floor. Butting each upper panel horizontally against the ceiling on long runs of wall, start about 12 inches from the top and drive $1\frac{1}{2}$-inch screws into joists at 12-inch intervals *(above)*.

2 Cut openings for windows and doors with a drywall saw *(above)*. Avoid making joints between panels at the edges of frames.

3 **Install panels vertically** on short runs of wall to avoid creating unnecessary joints. Hold a panel in place while screwing it using wood scraps as a foot lever *(above)*.

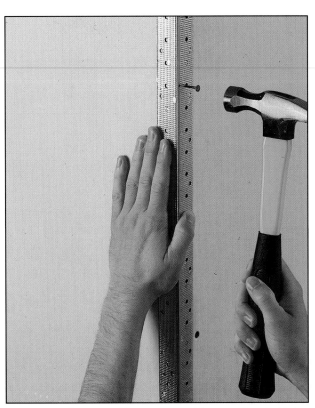

4 **Strengthen outside corners** with corner bead, driving $1\frac{1}{2}$-inch nails through the flanges *(above)*. (Screws may be used, but their heads are more difficult to conceal.)

CONCEALING WITH COMPOUND

Fasteners. With a 5-inch putty knife, cover fastener heads with joint compound *(above)* and scrape off excess. Let the compound dry, then make a pass with an 8-inch knife.

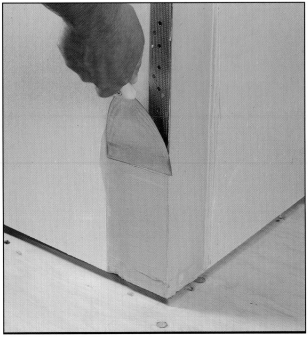

Corner bead. Apply a band of joint compound with a 5-inch putty knife along each side of the corner bead *(above)*. When the compound dries, make a pass with an 8-inch knife.

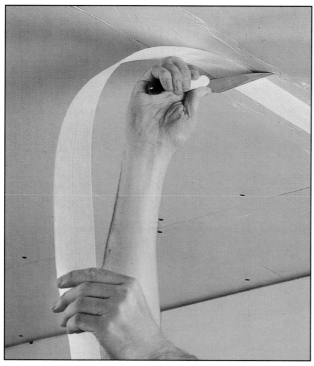
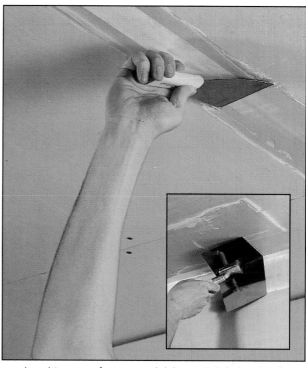

Joints and inside corners. With a 5-inch putty knife, cover each joint with a thin layer of joint compound and press into it a length of joint tape *(above, left)*. Embed the tape with another thin coat of compound *(above, right)*, then let the joint dry. For inside corners, crease the tape along the center and use a corner trowel to apply compound *(inset)*.

Feathering and sanding. Make a final pass with a 10-inch drywall knife along each side of joints, bearing on the blade's outside edge to spread and feather joint compound *(above, left)*. Apply compound and feather edges at corners and fasteners with an 8-inch putty knife. Let the compound dry, then sand using a swivel-mounted sanding plate *(above, right)* or a sanding block, or smooth with a damp drywall sponge *(inset)*.

30 Repairing Drywall Holes
$ Estimated Savings: $30

WHAT YOU NEED

Tools
- ✔ Utility knife
- ✔ Scissors
- ✔ Putty knives: 2-inch and 6-inch
- ✔ Sanding block

Materials
- ✔ Wire mesh
- ✔ String
- ✔ Pencil
- ✔ Joint compound
- ✔ Sandpaper

BEFORE YOU START

◆ Take action—preventive as well as remedial—to help reduce the likelihood of accidental or inadvertent holes being made. Be sure that all doors, for example, are equipped with doorstops.

◆ When relocating pictures and other wall hangings, disguise the tiny nail holes left behind by filling them with dabs of toothpaste.

◆ Stuff punctures up to 2 inches in size using a backing of balled-up newspaper. Holes more than 6 inches across are too large to be repaired with backing and compound; they require patching with drywall.

◆ Sanding joint compound generates a tremendous amount of tiny airborne dust particles that are difficult to clean up. Seal off the work area from other rooms to the fullest extent possible and clear away or drape plastic sheets over furnishings and appliances.

SAFETY FIRST

Wear a dust mask when sanding joint compound.

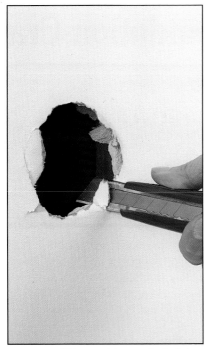

1 **Trim off loose bits** at the hole's edges using a utility knife *(above)*. Roughen the inside surface around the hole with coarse sandpaper.

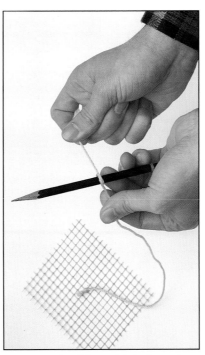

2 **Cut a backing** of $\frac{1}{4}$-inch mesh about 2 inches larger than the hole. Tie a length of string to the center of the backing and knot the other end to a pencil *(above)*.

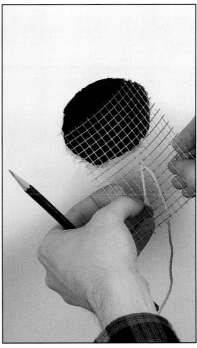

3 **Work the backing** into the hole *(above)*, keeping a grip on the pencil. Then, dampen the inside surface around the hole with water.

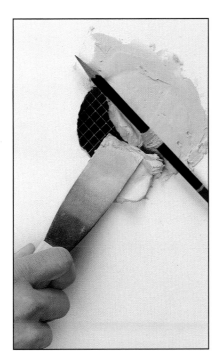

4 **Apply joint compound** to the hole's inside edges using a 2-inch putty knife, then pull the backing flat. Wrap the pencil with the slack string and twist it to brace the backing while packing in compound *(above)*.

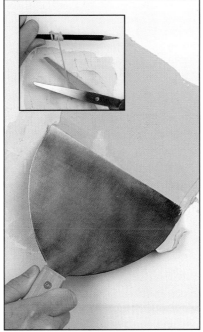

5 **Cut the string** to remove the pencil *(inset)* when the compound has dried. Dampen the patch, then use a 6-inch putty knife to apply a second coat of compound *(above)* and feather the edges of the repair.

6 **Smooth the surface** after the final coat dries using fine-grit sandpaper on a sanding block *(above)* and brush or wipe off dust. Seal the repair with primer before painting.

31 Repairing Interior Foundation Cracks

💲 Estimated Savings: $60

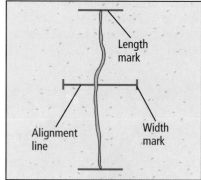

Hairline crack

Open crack

BEFORE YOU START

Uneven settlement of a foundation can result in serious cracks in a wall. Consult a building professional about any crack that:

◆ Runs vertically along or horizontally across a corner.

◆ Tapers along its length, or has edges that seem misaligned or different from each other in shape or position.

◆ Has a width greater than $\frac{1}{8}$ inch.

◆ Runs 3 feet or longer and lengthens by more than 25 percent in one year.

Monitoring a Crack

Length mark

Alignment line

Width mark

Make a length mark at each end of the crack, then draw an alignment line at a 90° angle across the center of the crack and make a width mark at each end of the line *(above)*. Measure and record the distances between the length and width marks, then remeasure the crack monthly for 6 to 12 months. If the crack is stable, patch it as a stationary crack. If the crack widens and narrows, patch it as a moving crack.

WHAT YOU NEED

HAIRLINE CRACK
Tools
✔ Fiber brush
✔ Putty knife
Materials
✔ Latex patching compound

STATIONARY OPEN CRACK
Tools
✔ Cold chisel
✔ Ball-peen hammer
✔ Fiber brush
✔ Paintbrush
✔ Putty knife or pointing trowel
✔ Mason's hawk
✔ Whisk broom
Materials
✔ Bonding agent
✔ Latex patching compound
✔ Plastic
✔ Duct tape

MOVING OPEN CRACK
Tools
✔ Cold chisel
✔ Ball-peen hammer
✔ Fiber brush
✔ Caulking gun
✔ Putty knife or pointing trowel
Materials
✔ Foam backing rod
✔ Elastomeric sealant

LEAKING CRACK
Tools
✔ Cold chisel
✔ Ball-peen hammer
✔ Fiber brush
✔ Putty knife or pointing trowel
Materials
✔ Hydraulic cement

✋ SAFETY FIRST

Wear safety goggles and a dust mask when cleaning and chiseling a crack.

HAIRLINE CRACK

1 Clean dirt and particles out of the crack with a fiber brush *(above)*. If recommended by the patching compound manufacturer, apply a bonding agent using a paintbrush.

2 Mix enough compound for the job. Pack the compound into the crack using a putty knife *(above)* or pointing trowel, overfilling it slightly.

3 Scrape off excess compound and feather the edges of the patch *(above)*. Until the compound cures, keep the patch moist by misting it with water when the edges lighten.

STATIONARY OPEN CRACK

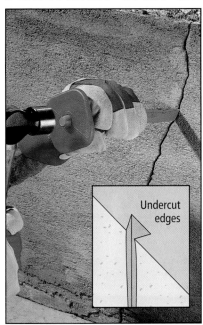

Undercut edges

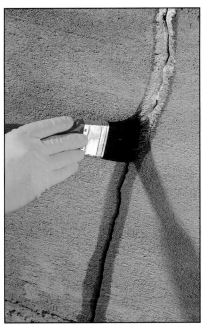

Mason's hawk

1 Widen the crack to $\frac{1}{4}$ inch and deepen it to $\frac{1}{2}$ inch using a cold chisel and ball-peen hammer *(above)*, undercutting *(inset)* or squaring the edges. Sweep the crack clean with a fiber brush.

2 Brush a bonding agent into the crack *(above)* to help the patching compound adhere. (Soaking the crack with water first may be recommended by the manufacturer.) Let the bonding agent set—usually about 15 minutes.

3 Prepare the compound on a mason's hawk or a board and pack it into the crack with a pointing trowel or putty knife. Work from the bottom to the top of the crack, overfilling it slightly *(above)*.

  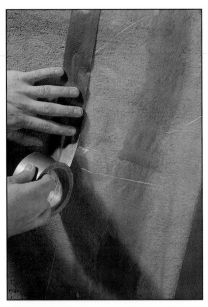

4 **Working from the top** to the bottom of the patch, scrape off excess compound *(above)*. Smooth the patch and feather the edges by drawing the trowel or knife firmly along the surface in a slight curving motion.

5 **Texture the patch** to match the surrounding surface using a whisk broom. Sweep the bristle tips of the broom lightly over the patch *(above)* to achieve the desired effect.

6 **Tape plastic** over the patch *(above)* to seal in moisture until the compound cures. Mist behind the plastic with water if the edges of the patch lighten prematurely.

MOVING OPEN CRACK

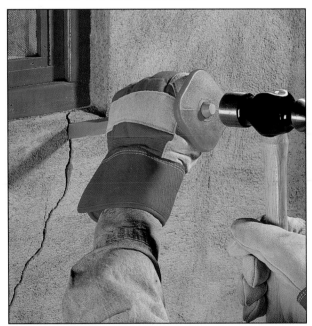 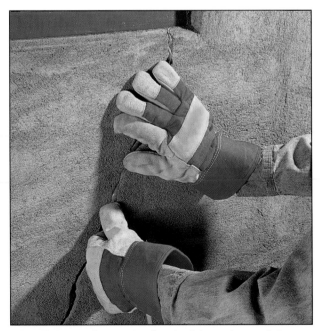

1 **Chip off loose** or crumbling bits with a cold chisel and ball-peen hammer, then widen and deepen the crack to at least $\frac{1}{4}$ inch *(above)*. Undercut or square the edges; don't taper them into a V shape. Clean the crack using a fiber brush.

2 **Fill the crack** to within $\frac{1}{4}$ inch of the surface with foam backing rod *(above)*; if the crack is less than $\frac{1}{2}$ inch deep, substitute wax paper. Press the filler to the full depth of the crack using a putty knife.

3 **Load a caulking gun** with elastomeric sealant. Holding the gun at a 45° angle to the surface, work from the top to the bottom of the crack to fill it *(above)*.

4 **Draw the wet blade** of a putty knife or pointing trowel along the patch to scrape off excess sealant and smooth it flush with the surrounding surface *(above)*. Let the sealant cure for the time specified by the manufacturer.

LEAKING CRACK

1 **Enlarge the crack** to a width and depth of at least $\frac{3}{4}$ inch using a cold chisel and ball-peen hammer. Work from the driest to the wettest point of the crack to pack it with hydraulic cement *(above)*. **Caution:** Wear rubber gloves to prevent skin contact with the cement.

2 **Fill the wettest spot** of the crack with a ball of cement molded into a cone-shaped plug *(above)*. Hold the plug in place until it sets—usually about 3 minutes. Smooth the patch with a putty knife or pointing trowel. Later, find the exterior origin of the leak and remedy it.

EXTERIOR

REPAIRS AND IMPROVEMENTS

PROJECT		PAGE
32	Painting Exterior Window Trim	112
33	Maintaining Gutters & Downspouts	116
34	Repairing Gutters & Downspouts	118
35	Replacing Asphalt Shingles	122
36	Waterproofing Brick & Cement	128
37	Replacing Window Screens	130
38	Installing a Prehung Window	132
39	Replacing a Window Pane	136
40	Adding Locks to Windows	140
41	Adding a Deadbolt Lockset	142

32 Painting Exterior Window Trim

$ Estimated Savings: $60

BEFORE YOU START

◆ Decide how much primer and paint you will need. The average window will need about 1 pint per coat. Have enough primer for one coat and paint for two coats.

◆ Read labels before opening cans.

◆ Paint when humidity is low, especially with oil-based paints.

◆ Paint in temperatures above 50°F, and in the shade if possible.

◆ If insects invade your paint, spray insect repellent on the paint. That small amount will not affect or discolor it.

WHAT YOU NEED

Tools
- ✔ Container for mixing paint
- ✔ Paint paddle
- ✔ Nail set
- ✔ 2-inch angled paint brush
- ✔ Putty knife
- ✔ Caulking gun
- ✔ Window scraper

Materials
- ✔ Fine- and medium-grit sandpaper
- ✔ Masking tape
- ✔ Primer
- ✔ Wood filler
- ✔ Paint

"BOXING" PAINT: To ensure maximum coverage you should box your paint even if it has been premixed at the store.

(1) Pour the top $\frac{1}{3}$ of the paint—the thinnest portion —into a pail.

(2) Use a paddle to stir any paint that has settled in the bottom of the can.

(3) Continue stirring and gradually return all of the paint back to the original can.

(4) Pour it back and forth between containers until it is uniform in consistency.

✋ SAFETY FIRST

The paint in old homes (before 1978) may contain lead. Test a flake with a kit available at hardware stores. If lead is present, check with your local health department or environmental protection office for precautions.

PREPARING NEW SURFACES FOR PAINT

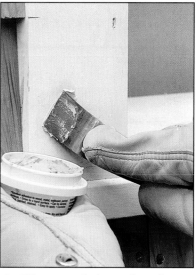

1 **Sand rough surfaces** and splintered edges with fine-grit paper *(above)*. Countersink protruding nails and prepare the surface following instructions in *Preparing Surfaces for Paint & Wallpaper* (page 50).

2 **Wash off dirt** *(above)* with a solution of $\frac{1}{3}$ cup powdered detergent per gallon of warm water. If there are signs of mildew, which will bleed through paint, add $\frac{1}{2}$ cup bleach to the solution.

3 **Fill gouges, holes and cracks** with wood filler. Allow filler to dry (see container for drying times), then sand even. Apply a coat of primer on bare wood and any filled or sanded areas.

PREPARING WEATHERED OR DAMAGED SURFACES

Remove loose paint with a scraper or rasp tool *(above)* and finish off with a wire brush. Use a nylon paint stripper fitted to an electric drill or a heat gun to remove many layers of paint. When removing paint near glass, use a chemical paint stripper to prevent breakage. Replace loose or damaged glazing and glass—see *Replacing a Window Pane* (page 130).

Sand all surfaces with medium-grit sandpaper then proceed to fine-grit paper. For muntins, fold a 6-inch square of sandpaper into quarters to make a sharp sanding edge *(above)*. Place the edge against the surface and rub gently to blend the edges of patching material or old paint with the surrounding surface. Brush off dust and dirt before repainting.

Look along the space where the window trim meets the shingles or siding. If you see an open crack, run a bead of exterior caulking compound inside the crack *(above)* to seal the joints and prevent air leaks. Purchase an inexpensive caulking gun and a tube of vinyl adhesive caulk, which goes on white but will dry clear. Cut the nozzle to the width of the crack.

PAINTING SASHES AND TRIM

A FEATHERED BRUSH STROKE

Make the length of each stroke about double the length of the bristles. Wherever possible, end the stroke in the wet paint of a previously painted section. (1) Start the brush stroke with the flat side of the brush slightly angled low to the surface. (2) As you move the brush, increase the angle gradually. (3) End the stroke by drawing the brush up and off the surface with a slight twist; the brush should leave a thin, feathered edge of paint. If one stroke covers the surface satisfactorily, move on to an adjacent area. Otherwise, repaint the area with a second stroke.

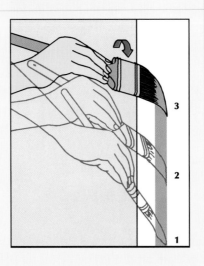

1 **Use semi-gloss,** exterior trim paint. If the paint is too thick to flow into corners, thin it as directed on the label. Apply two coats with a light sanding between them. To avoid ridges and lap marks stroke from dry to wet.

2 **Lower the outside sash** and raise the inside one, essentially reversing their positions as far as they will go without force. If there are muntins, paint them first. Painting onto the glass is good—it seals the rubber or puttied filler between the glass and the frame. Tape before you paint *(above)* or scrape paint off after.

Stile

3 **Paint the face** of the inside sash's upper rail but not its top edge because that is the color of the interior trim. Paint as far down the side stiles *(above)* as you can reach easily. Paint all of the outside sash. Paint its top edge now because it will be difficult to reach later.

4 **Return both sashes** to their normal closed position but leave about a 1-inch gap top and bottom so the wet paint will not seal the frames shut when it dries. Finish the stiles and bottom rail of the inside sash. Paint the bottom of the outside rail. Don't close the sashes until they dry.

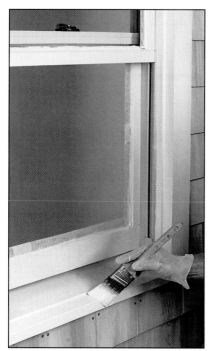

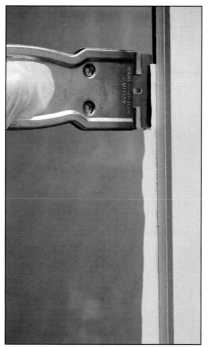

5 **Paint the trim,** starting across the top and then working down each side, doing the jambs as you go. Paint strokes on the header should be horizontal, following the grain of the wood. If the channels are plastic, don't paint them; if raw wood, paint them with plain linseed oil. Do the sill last *(above)* to wipe up any drips from the top.

6 **Clean up promptly.** The longer paint dries, the more difficult it is to remove. Remove masking tape when the paint is dry, but still tacky. Tape removed too soon could smear the paint; left too long it will stick and tear. When the paint has dried completely, use a window scraper *(above)* to remove spots of paint or tape.

Newer windows are often made with solid, double-pane, thermal glass. If a "Colonial" style home demands small panes, a simulated muntin-grid can produce a similar effect. The wood or plastic grid fits against the glass on the inside. Paint the out-facing surface the same color as the exterior window frame.

CLEANING CONTAMINANTS FROM PAINT

Removing paint skin

Purchase paper paint strainers. They look like large coffee filters. They are made in fine and medium mesh and sold in packages of four. Gently separate the skin from the side of the paint can with a paddle. Hold the filter over a clean container. Pour the paint through it *(left)*, then discard the filter. Mix the remaining paint. The newly filtered paint will not be affected by the loss of the material in the skin.

Keeping the paint clean

This method is simpler than trying to fish out a brush bristle or other contaminant that falls in. Cut a piece of window screening to the size of the paint pail opening. Drop the screen onto the surface *(right)*. The screen will sink, taking any debris to the bottom and trapping it there.

33 Maintaining Gutters & Downspouts
💲 Estimated Savings: $30

BEFORE YOU START

◆ Work only in good weather conditions—never when it is wet or windy.

◆ Reduce the number of trips up and down the ladder by having a helper pass tools and turn water on and off.

◆ Place a 2-by-4 in the gutter to keep it from being crushed by the ladder.

WHAT YOU NEED

Tools
- ✔ Extension ladder
- ✔ Garden hose and nozzle
- ✔ Whisk broom

🛑 SAFETY FIRST

Keep your hips between the rails of the ladder; don't overreach.

PREVENTIVE MAINTENANCE

Hanger

Screen out leaves to reduce routine cleaning. Seat a leaf strainer in the drop outlet of each downspout *(left)*. Fit vinyl gutters with plastic snap-on leaf guard *(above, left)*. For aluminum gutters, install rolled lengths of wide-mesh metal leaf guard; slip the guard under hangers *(above, right)* or notch it to rest on them.

1 **Handpick leaves,** twigs and other debris out of the open gutter *(above)* and from along the roof edge. Wear rubber gloves to keep your hands clean and bag collected debris for disposal.

2 **Flush the downspout** with water to clear it. Aim the hose into the drop outlet *(above)*, washing debris and grit down through the elbow and out the bottom of the downspout.

3 **Wash the gutter** with a garden hose, sweeping dirt and grit toward the downspout with a whisk broom *(above)*. Put a nozzle on the hose so the water pressure and spray can be adjusted.

CLOGGED DOWNSPOUT

Clear a clog with a trap-and-drain auger. Push the auger's coil into the drop outlet and as far as possible through the elbow, then lock the handle and turn it clockwise *(above)*. When the handle turns easily, unlock it and feed the coil farther down.

34 Repairing Gutters & Downspouts

$ Estimated Savings: $60

BEFORE YOU START

◆ Tears or holes in aluminum or vinyl gutters cannot be effectively repaired. Replace the full section.

◆ Replace the entire length of a seamless aluminum gutter. Check the local Yellow Pages under "gutters" for a dealer. Piecing together the 10-foot lengths commonly available in stores will not eliminate leaks and sags.

◆ Elbows are made at different angles so take the damaged one with you when you buy a replacement for it.

◆ There are two ways gutters are attached. **Old:** A spike fits through the hole in the front lip of the gutter, through a loose sleeve the width of the gutter, and is driven through the back lip of the gutter and into the wood trim or rafter behind it. **New:** Newer bracket systems are more secure. A spring-steel strap tucks under the outer lip of gutter and underneath the bottom to be screwed (not nailed) into the trim or rafter on the back side.

TIP

To determine whether a gutter is bent out of alignment, hose water onto the roof, directing the spray from side to side. Watch the flow of water in the gutter to see if it runs **away** from the downspout or collects in a sag.

WHAT YOU NEED

Tools
- ✔ Hose
- ✔ Ladder
- ✔ Claw hammer
- ✔ Screwdriver
- ✔ Lock-grip pliers
- ✔ Small flat pry-bar
- ✔ Drain auger
- ✔ Caulking gun
- ✔ Wire brush
- ✔ Putty knife
- ✔ Strong rubber gloves
- ✔ Pocket square
- ✔ Hand saw

Materials
- ✔ Replacement gutter and down-spout, straps, elbows and fasteners
- ✔ Epoxy
- ✔ Vinyl adhesive caulk

SAFETY FIRST

Take caution when working from a ladder. Do not lean the ladder against a metal gutter, which could bend and give way.

ADJUSTING METAL GUTTERS TO SLOPE CORRECTLY

1 **Determine which way the water** flows from roof runoff. (See Tip on page 118.) When a sagging gutter has a downspout at both ends of its length, you need only raise the center-point enough so water flows away from it.

2 **Remove the gutter support** at the point where water starts to flow away from the downspout. Unscrew or pull out the nail that attaches the bracket to the fascia *(above)*. Replace the old brackets; they are seldom worth saving.

3 **To remove a spike,** grab the head with locking-grip pliers and work it free. If it sticks slide the nail-pulling teeth of a flat pry-bar under the lip of the gutter next to the nail. Hit the curved back *(above)* to drive the head through the lip of the gutter. Replace the spike with a bracket system.

4 **Raise the gutter by hand** while an assistant sprays water into the gutter. When water begins to flow toward the downspout, mark the fascia board *(above)* where the rafter meets it. Reposition the gutter support at that point.

FIXING DAMAGED DOWNSPOUTS

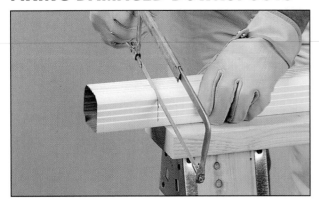

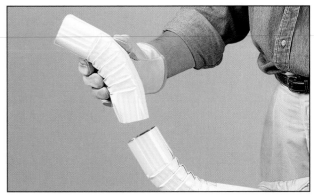

1 **If a metal or vinyl downspout** is bent or torn, remove and replace it with a new one. Buy a new 10-foot section of downspout. Measure and cut its length to align with whatever water-runoff system its bottom end will fit into.

2 **Install an elbow** at the top and bottom of the downspout to line up with the drain hole in the gutter. Attach straps and fasten it in position vertically. See page 188 for more information on drainage and a drywell outflow system.

UNCLOGGING A DOWNSPOUT

If a downspout is not damaged but water is not flowing through it, the chances are good that it is clogged with debris. Without removing the downspout, snake a plumber's drain auger down inside the downspout then lock the handle. Crank the handle clockwise to loosen the obstruction. Flush the downspout through with a hose. If the gutter is only tilted incorrectly, remove the incorrectly positioned strap or spike and replace it with a new one, aligning the downspout under the gutter's drain hole.

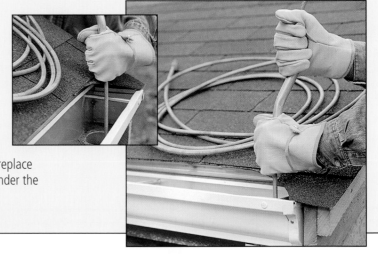

REPAIRING SMALL HOLES OR CRACKS IN WOODEN GUTTERS

1 **Clean the inner surface of a leaky gutter** with a wire brush *(above)* to locate the damage. Water can stream or drip through holes or splits. Usually it runs down the bottom of the gutter to a low spot before it runs off.

2 **Cut away remaining rot and debris** in and around the damaged area inside the gutter. Cut a V-shaped channel of bare wood inside a split or crack. Mix epoxy and fill the channel. Don't try to fill holes bigger than a pin.

REPLACING ROTTED OR BROKEN SECTIONS OF WOODEN GUTTERS

1 **Without removing the gutter,** use a combination square to mark or scribe parallel 45° angles at each end of the damaged area.

2 **Cut through the gutter** from the bottom with a hand saw *(above)* following the 45° marks. (Professionals use a power "sawsall" tool.) Remove the damaged section.

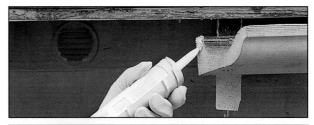

3 **Lay the damaged section** on a new length of gutter. With a straightedge trace along the angled cut(s) onto the new length. Cut the matching piece, adjusting for the width of the straightedge. Drill a downspout hole, if necessary.

4 **Fit the new piece** in place. Adjust the angle with a saw or rasp if necessary. Coat one cut with caulk and refasten it through the original holes, using screws or 6d galvanized wood nails.

Replacing a gutter endcap.
The cap at the end of a gutter often rots away. Replace it with lead sheet. With a utility knife, cut a square piece of sheet lead slightly larger than the gutter's profile. Smear enough caulk on the gutter-end to squeeze a bead out around the inside seam. Nail through the lead into the gutter-end all around *(left)*, using roofing nails. Trim away extra lead around the gutter-end. With your fingertip, smooth the bead of caulk into the inside seams so it won't act like a water-dam. Smooth the outside bead, if any, for looks.

Replacing the turnaround.
A wooden gutter is usually finished by turning the corner of the roof with the fascia board onto the gable end where the downspout is attached. The seams rot and leak when water collects. Remove the old pieces carefully enough to use them as patterns to construct new ones. Glue and nail the new pieces together. Set and fill the nail holes and caulk the inside seams as described for the endcap *(far left)* before nailing the new endcap in place. Nail in or near the old holes into the ends of the rafters.

35 Replacing Asphalt Shingles
$ Estimated Savings: $30 per 100 sq. ft.

BEFORE YOU START

◆ Plan repairs for a dry, calm day without hot sunshine. Never go up onto the roof in cold, wet or windy weather.

◆ If the roof is steeper than a vertical rise of 6 inches in a horizontal run of 12 inches—a pitch of more than 6 in 12—have the necessary repairs done by a roofing professional.

◆ Set up to work on the roof so that there is no need to walk diagonally up and down a slope; whenever possible, walk only straight up and down it.

◆ If desired, wear an approved safety belt or harness; follow the manufacturer's instructions to anchor it securely.

SAFETY FIRST

Wear work boots or sturdy shoes that feature well-defined heels and nonslip rubber soles. Wear safety goggles to drive nails. Avoid skin contact with roofing cement by wearing work gloves.

WHAT YOU NEED

Tools
✔ Pry bar
✔ Putty knife or pointing trowel

✔ Claw hammer
✔ Tin snips
Materials
✔ Shingles

✔ Building paper
✔ Roofing cement
✔ Roofing nails

1 **Remove damaged shingles** one course at a time, working top to bottom. To find nails holding a shingle, lift tabs one course *(above, top)* and two courses above it. (Loosen edges with a putty knife.) Slip a pry bar under the shingle to raise each nail head, then slide the pry bar out to pull out the nails *(above, bottom)*.

2 **With a putty knife** or pointing trowel, fill nail holes and seal small tears in the building paper with roofing cement *(above)*. For larger holes, nail a patch of building paper in place and apply a small dab of roofing cement on each nail head.

SINGLE TAB

To replace one tab on a shingle, pull out nails under tabs one and two courses above it, then cut it off with tin snips *(below, top)*. Apply roofing cement *(below, center)*, then nail the replacement tab into place just below the self-sealing adhesive about 1 inch from each end *(below, bottom)*. Replace the nails under tabs one and two courses above the new tab, then cover the nail heads and seal the corners of the tabs with roofing cement.

New tab

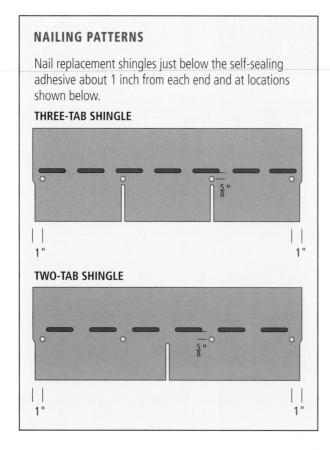

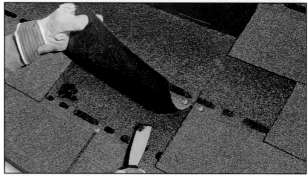

3 **Working bottom to top** one course at a time, slide the replacement shingles into position and nail them *(above, top)*. Apply a small dab of roofing cement under the shingles about 2 inches from the corners of each tab *(above, bottom)*, then press the tabs into place.

4 **Slide each shingle** of the last course into position under tabs one course above it *(above, left)*. (Trim the top of a shingle with tin snips, if necessary, to fit it.) Nail the shingle into place and seal the corners of each tab with roof-ing cement. Replace the nails under tabs one course and two courses above the new shingle *(above, center)*, then cover the nail heads and seal the corners of the tabs with roofing cement *(above, right)*.

EDGES AND PEAKS

Eaves and rakes. Remove shingles and nails as needed to replace any damaged starter shingles at eaves and rakes. For an eave, make a replacement starter shingle by cutting the tabs off a shingle just below the self-sealing adhesive, then position it *(above, left)* and apply a band of roofing cement 3 inches wide under its outer edge. For a rake, slide a full-size shingle into place with its top at the outer edge *(above, right)*. Nail starter shingles 3 to 4 inches from the edge about 1 inch from each end and at intervals of 10 inches. Replace shingles and nails removed to reach starter shingles.

Ridges and hips. To remove a damaged shingle at a ridge or hip, pull out nails under shingles one and two courses above it. Make a replacement shingle by cutting off a tab 12 inches square and tapering the top 1 inch from each edge to about $\frac{1}{2}$ inch below the self-sealing adhesive *(above, left)*. Slide the shingle into place and nail it just below the adhesive 1 inch from each end *(above, right)*. Replace the nails under shingles one and two courses above the new shingle, then seal the corners of the shingles with roofing cement.

125

VALLEYS

Flashing

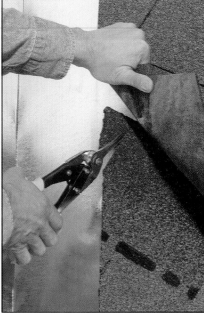

Open valley. Slide a shingle into position at an inside corner with exposed flashing so that it overhangs the valley. With tin snips, trim the shingle using the courses above and below it as guides *(above, left)*, then snip about 1 inch off the top corner at a 45° angle *(above, center)*. Apply a band of roofing cement 3 inches wide under the trimmed edge of the shingle, then secure it with nails 6 inches from the center of the valley *(above, right)* and seal the tabs.

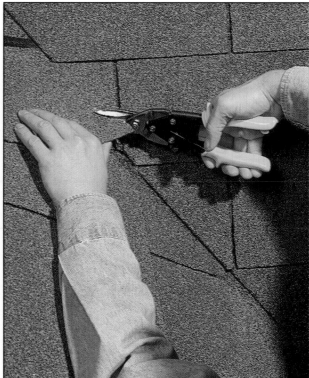

Closed cut valley. At an inside corner without exposed flashing, slide a shingle into position so that it overlaps the valley *(above, left)*. Trim the shingle using the courses above and below it as guides *(above, right)*, then snip about 1 inch off the top corner at a 45° angle. Apply a band of roofing cement 3 inches wide under the trimmed edge of the shingle, then secure it with nails 6 inches from the center of the valley and seal the tabs.

OBSTRUCTIONS

Above a vent. Slide a shingle into place above a vent so that it overlaps the flashing, then trim it to fit snugly and lie flat *(above, left)*. Seal the bottom edge of the shingle onto the flashing with a band of roofing cement 3 inches wide *(above, right)*, then secure it with nails at least 2 inches from the flashing and seal the corners of the tabs.

Below a vent. To position a shingle below a vent, pry up the flashing and pull out the nails securing it *(above, left)*. Cut a shingle to fit snugly around the vent using tin snips, then slide it into place under the flashing *(above, right)*. Seal the flashing to the shingle with a 3-inch band of roofing cement, then secure the shingle with nails at least 2 inches from the flashing and seal the corners of the tabs. Replace the nails pulled out of the flashing and apply a small dab of roofing cement on each nail head.

36 Waterproofing Brick & Cement
$ Estimated Savings: $150

BEFORE YOU START
◆ Waterproofing the exterior surface of a chimney or an above-grade foundation wall by filling cracks and applying liquid sealant can prevent moisture from seeping through and "weeping" on the inside. This process also prevents salts, lime and other materials in the wall from bleeding to the surface, drying there and causing unsightly stains.

◆ If water is seeping through a foundation the best solution is to divert the source. See *Controlling Ground Water Runoff* (page 188).

◆ It is best to buy commercial liquid sealants and cleaners from a drywall and masonry supplies dealer.

◆ Sealants are a mix of silicones in a volatile liquid that penetrates brick and concrete. The liquid evaporates leaving the silicone plugging the pores. Modern formulas are not as potentially explosive or polluting as the old alcohol- or petroleum-based sealants.

CLEANING BEFORE SEALING
The most common problem on brick is efflorescence *(below)*—a white stain from natural salts or alkaline in the brick and mortar that seeps to the surface. Remove stains before sealing.

Use a premixed muriatic (hydrochloric) acid, water-soluble cleaner, available at home centers and drywall-masonry supply dealers. Follow instructions on the label and allow it to dry completely before sealing.

Some commercial cleaners even soften fresh spills of mortar. If on brick, apply the cleaner and scrape the mortar off with an old piece of brick. If the mortar is not completely removed the brick will color it.

WHAT YOU NEED

Tools
- ✔ Brush
- ✔ Applicator, roller or pump
- ✔ Mason's tools

Materials
- ✔ Mortar and caulking gun
- ✔ Masonry and brick cleaner
- ✔ Siloxane water repellent

SAFETY FIRST

Wear protective clothing, goggles and gloves when using sealants.

1 **Look for holes in the mortar** in brick chimneys and walls. Look for cracks in the concrete "caps" around the tops of chimney flues. Chip away crumbling masonry and open cracks in masonry with a mason's chisel *(above)*.

2 **Fill widened cracks and holes** with an acrylic mortar compound in a caulking tube *(above, left)*, which is easier than mixing a batch of mortar. Smooth joints with a pointing tool *(above, right)*. Seal thin cracks with clear silicone.

3 **Mix a pailful** of water-based silane/siloxane water repellent for masonry surfaces. Spread a drop cloth over vegetation near the foundation to be sealed *(above)*. Also protect asphalt shingles. Wash spills and spatter off tools and uncovered surfaces immediately.

4 **Apply sealer,** following directions on the label, using a lamb's wool applicator *(above)*, roller or low-pressure spray (see page 128, top). Wear rubber gloves, goggles, protective clothing and an organic respirator (page 196) as advised by precautions on the container.

37 Replacing Window Screens
💲 Estimated Savings: $30

BEFORE YOU START
◆ Remove the frame from the window or door to work on the screen.
◆ To clean screening, use a vacuum. Rub with steel wool to remove rust.

Gluing a Small Tear

Align the strands and apply a small dab of waterproof glue with a toothpick *(above)*. Hold the strands in place until the glue sets.

WHAT YOU NEED

Tools
✔ Screwdriver
✔ Scissors
✔ Utility knife
✔ Spline roller
Materials
✔ Replacement screening
✔ Spline

ALUMINUM PATCH
Trim the hole and cut a patch large enough to cover it. Sew the patch in place *(near right)* with transparent nylon thread (dark thread is shown for clarity). Or, pull out a few of the strands along each side of the patch and use a straightedge to bend the remaining strands at a right angle. Work the bent strands through the screening, then bend them down to secure the patch *(far right)*.

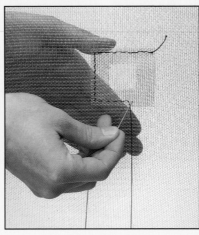

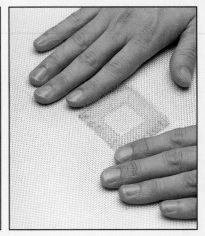

FIBERGLASS PATCH

Snip off loose strands and cut a patch larger than the hole. Coat the edges of the patch with waterproof glue *(above, top)* and press it into place. Alternatively, position the patch and cover it with a cotton cloth, then fuse it in place using the heat of an iron *(above, bottom)*.

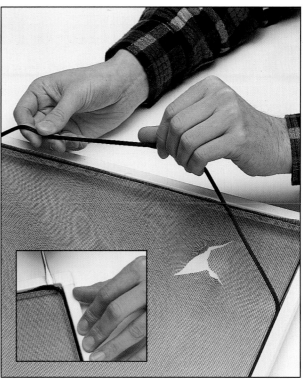

1 **Pry the spline** out of one corner of the frame with a screwdriver *(inset)*, then work around the frame to pull it free *(above)*. (If planning to reuse the spline, be careful not to stretch or tear it.) Remove the screening, then cut a replacement panel several inches larger than the frame.

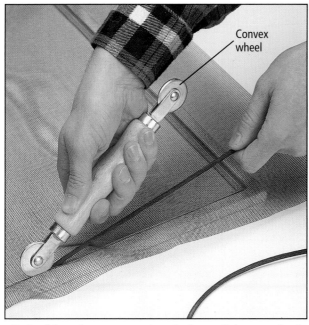

Convex wheel

2 **Position the new panel** on the frame. If the screening is fiberglass, force the spline and screening together into the channel with the concave wheel of a spline roller *(above)*. Press aluminum screening into the channel using the roller's convex wheel before forcing in the spline.

3 **Trim off excess screening** by running a utility knife along the outside edges of the frame's channel *(above)*. Cut off the surplus spline, then tuck the ends into the channel firmly with a screwdriver.

38 Installing a Prehung Window
💲 Estimated Savings: $120

BEFORE YOU START

When measuring for a new window, take each dimension at three different places and note the smallest readings.

Window Frame

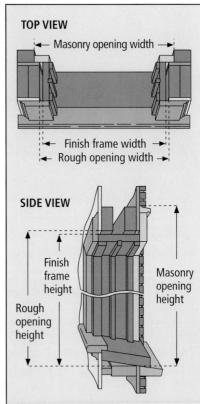

TOP VIEW

◀— Masonry opening width —▶

◀— Finish frame width —▶
◀— Rough opening width —▶

SIDE VIEW

Finish frame height

Rough opening height

Masonry opening height

◆ Most prehung windows are built for installing in the rough opening—which is usually about $\frac{1}{2}$ inch larger in width and height than the finish frame.

◆ Also measure the masonry opening for a prehung window when the exterior is brick, stone or other similar material.

SAFETY FIRST

Wear rubber gloves to avoid skin contact with fiberglass insulation.

WHAT YOU NEED

Tools
- ✔ Utility knife
- ✔ Utility bar
- ✔ Claw hammer
- ✔ Nail set
- ✔ Hacksaw
- ✔ Carpenter's level
- ✔ Staple gun

- ✔ Putty knife
- ✔ Caulking gun

Materials
- ✔ Prehung window
- ✔ Filament tape
- ✔ Filler strips
- ✔ Drip cap
- ✔ Wood shims

- ✔ Common nails
- ✔ Polyethylene vapor barrier
- ✔ Staples
- ✔ Finishing nails
- ✔ Insulation
- ✔ Jamb extensions
- ✔ Exterior caulk

1 **Slice through paint** sealing the interior trim with a utility knife. Gently pry off the trim *(above, left)*, using a wood shim as shown to protect the surrounding surface.

Remove the exterior trim *(above, right)* and pull nails through any trim that can be reused.

FLANGE-MOUNTED WINDOW

Cut free a window that is secured by flanges behind the siding using a saber saw with a metal-cutting blade *(below)*. If the new window also has flanges, trim $1\frac{3}{4}$ inches off the siding with a circular saw and remove the old window with its flanges intact.

2 **Drive nails through** the frame *(inset)* or cut them using the blade of a hacksaw. Lock the window and reinforce the panes of glass with nylon filament tape, then carefully lift the window out of the opening *(above)*.

3 **Block the rough frame** so that the opening is no more than $\frac{1}{2}$ inch higher and wider than the new window. Nail filler strips first to the bottom and top of the frame, then block the sides equally *(above)*.

4 **For an opening** in siding other than masonry, place a drip cap at the top to divert water. Cut the drip cap to length with a hacksaw, then insert it between the siding and sheathing *(above)*.

5 **Cut a vapor barrier** of polyethylene wider than the window frame and long enough to fit around it. Staple the vapor barrier to the frame so that the surplus overhangs on the interior side *(above)*.

Drip cap

6 **Lift the window frame** into the opening and under the drip cap *(above)*, then push it firmly into place. Tack the lower of the top corners with a finishing nail, then level the frame and tack the other top corner.

7 **Shim the window frame** inside at the bottom corners, along each side *(above)* and at the top; check for plumb and level, as shown. Secure the frame with finishing nails and countersink the heads, then trim the shims with a utility knife.

8 **Fill the gap** around the window frame with insulation *(above)*, then slip the vapor barrier into place behind the edges of the wall.

9 **If the jambs** of the window don't sit flush with the wall, add strips of wood to extend them *(above)*. Then, install the interior trim.

10 **Nail the exterior trim** to the window frame *(above)*, then seal the gap between the frame and the siding with exterior caulk.

39 Replacing a Window Pane
💲 Estimated Savings: $45

BEFORE YOU START

◆ To calculate the size of a replacement pane of glass, measure the inside height and width of the sash, then subtract $\frac{1}{8}$ inch from each dimension.

◆ Panes of glass in modern sashes may be installed with special moldings,

clips, gaskets or sealants. To be sure that replacement materials are compatible with both the new pane of glass and the sash, take along samples of the old materials to a window dealer or building supply center.

◆ As a stopgap measure when a broken pane of glass cannot be replaced immediately, clear away loose shards and fragments, then tape cardboard or heavy plastic in place over the opening in the sash.

WHAT YOU NEED

Tools
- ✔ Putty knife
- ✔ Soldering iron
- ✔ Long-nose pliers
- ✔ Wire brush

- ✔ Paintbrush

Materials
- ✔ Cardboard box
- ✔ Sandpaper
- ✔ Linseed oil

- ✔ Replacement glass pane
- ✔ Glazing compound
- ✔ Glazier's points
- ✔ Paint or varnish

✋ SAFETY FIRST

Wear heavy-duty work gloves when handling glass.
Prevent eye injury from flying shards by wearing safety goggles.

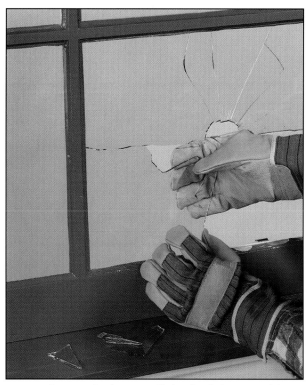

1 **Wearing work gloves,** pull shards of glass out of the sash *(above)*; gently wiggle stubborn fragments to free them. Place the broken glass in a cardboard box for disposal.

2 **Pry glazing compound** out of the sash with a putty knife *(above)*. Soften hardened compound, if necessary, by heating it with the tip of a soldering iron *(inset)*.

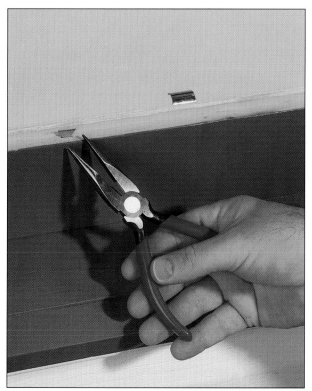

3 **Pull glazier's points** out of the sash with long-nose pliers *(above)*. Clean the sash channel using a wire brush, then smooth it with medium sandpaper.

4 **Prepare the sash channel** for putty-type glazing compound by brushing it with linseed oil *(above)*.

137

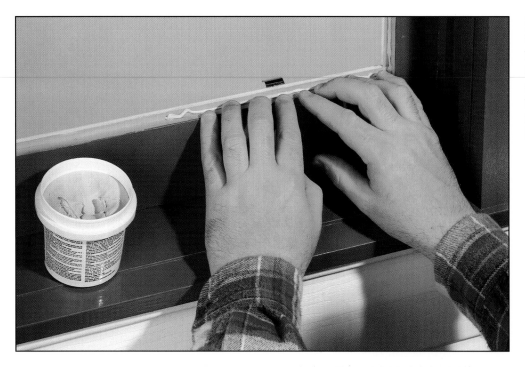

5 Line the sash channel with a thin bed of glazing compound, rolling a small amount at a time into a snake-like shape and pressing it into place *(left)*.

METAL SASHES

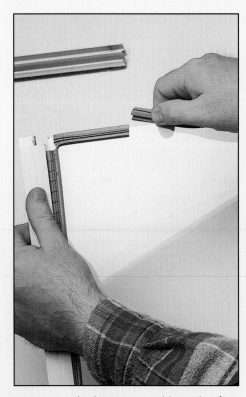

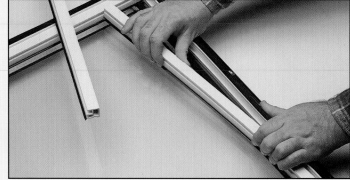

Unscrew and take apart an older style of metal sash to remove the rubber gasket around the pane of glass. Fit the rubber gasket around the replacement pane of glass and reassemble the sash *(above)*.

Unsnap the beveled moldings of a newer style of metal sash, then remove the pane of glass and glazing tape. Apply new glazing tape along the edges of the sash and peel off the backing *(above, top)*, then seat the replacement pane of glass and snap the moldings back into place *(above, bottom)*.

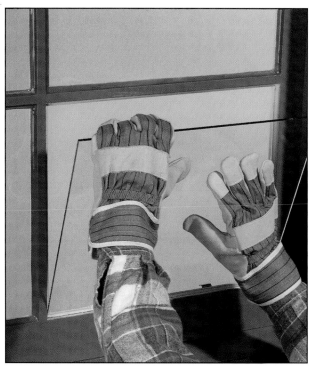

6 **Wearing work gloves,** carefully set the replacement pane of glass into the bed of glazing compound in the sash channel *(above)*; make sure that it is seated snugly.

7 **With a putty knife,** press glazier's points halfway into the sash and snug against the pane of glass at intervals of 4 to 6 inches *(above)*.

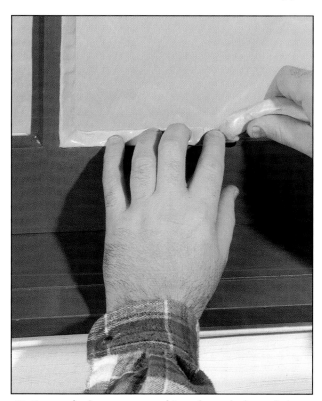

8 **Press glazing compound** into the sash channel along each edge of the pane of glass, beveling it at a 45° angle and embedding the glazier's points *(above)*.

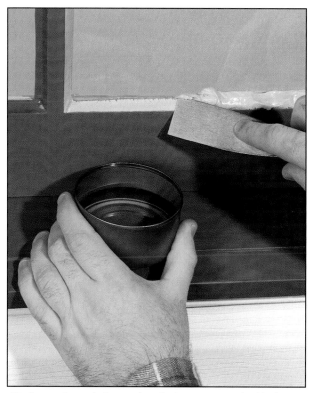

9 **Smooth and shape** the glazing compound with the wet blade of a putty knife *(above)*. Wipe off excess compound and let it set; when it no longer shows a thumbprint, apply paint or varnish.

40 Adding Locks to Windows
$ Estimated Savings: $60

BEFORE YOU START
◆ To determine which windows are most in need of extra security locks, take a tour of your dwelling from an intruder's perspective. Which windows are accessible from the ground or from adjoining structures? Are any windows hidden by bushes or trees?

◆ In addition to extra window locks, motion-sensitive floodlights positioned to illuminate dark outside areas can help (see *Installing a Motion Detector,* page 46).

◆ Window buzzers, set to sound an alarm whenever a window is opened, are available in kits you can easily install yourself.

◆ A dowel in the running track can prevent entry through sliders left slightly open at night for ventilation.

LOCKS FOR SASH WINDOWS
These locks are all for double-hung (sash) windows. Key locks similar to the rod lock shown above are available for hinged casement windows. The seats for rod locks can also be positioned to allow the window to be opened slightly for ventilation.

Lag bolt lock *(right)*
For double-hung (sash) windows, this works similarly to the home-made nail bolt or the rod lock; instead of a key, a lag bolt lock comes with a wrench to tighten and loosen the bolt.

Rod lock *(above)*
For double-hung (sash) windows, this type of lock works on the same principle as the nail in the sash, except that you use a key to remove the bolt. Similar key locks are available for hinged casement windows.

Nail in sash *(opposite page, top)*
A nail slipped into a downward-angled hole fixes the bottom and the top sash together, providing an inexpensive home-made lock for a sash window.

WHAT YOU NEED

Tools
✔ Drill and bits
✔ Phillips screwdriver
✔ Wire cutter
✔ Hammer

Materials
✔ For nail-in-sash lock: 3-inch nail, trim paint
✔ For bolt lock or rod lock: The hardware kits contain needed materials.

SAFETY FIRST

Wear safety goggles when operating an electric drill.

LOCKING A DOUBLE-HUNG WINDOW WITH A NAIL

1 Close the sashes completely. Drill a $\frac{3}{16}$-inch hole at a slight downward angle through the top rail of the inside sash and partly into the upper sash. A standard, 3-inch nail should easily drop into the hole.

2 Trim the head from the nail with wire cutters so that the nail is just out of reach when slipped into the hole, preventing an intruder from reaching in and removing the nail. Keep a magnet handy to retrieve the nail when you want to unlock the window *(above, left)*. Another solution is to leave the head on and paint the head of the nail the same color as the sash to make it less visible when it is pushed flush with the sash *(above, right)*.

FITTING A ROD LOCK

1 Position the lock, bolt extended, flush with the top rail of the bottom sash and as far from the glass as possible to avoid drilling into the glass. Tap the lock *(above, top)* to mark the location for the bolt hole.

2 Tape a drill bit at the depth the instructions specify for the bolt hole and drill it at the mark on the sash *(above, top)*. Extend the bolt into the hole. Mark and drill holes for the screws and mount the lock.

3 To allow ventilation, drill another hole 4 inches higher than the first *(above, top)*. If protective metal sleeves are supplied with the lock kit, insert one into each hole. Lock the rod into the top hole to allow air flow.

41 Adding a Deadbolt Lockset

💲 Estimated Savings: $70

DEADBOLT LOCKSET ANATOMY

Shown here is a single-cylinder deadbolt lockset.

Thumbturn

Drive bar

Cylinder assembly

Bolt assembly

Strike plate

BEFORE YOU START

◆ For a door with a window that could be broken to reach the interior side of a lock, consider buying a double-cylinder deadbolt lockset—which unlocks or locks from outdoors and indoors only by using a key. Check first that this type of lock is permitted by local building and fire codes; it may be prohibited for its potential to impede quick escape outdoors in an emergency.

◆ Install a deadbolt lockset at any convenient height on the door, but not less than 6 inches from the doorknob—a location where it might interfere with the handles of screen or storm doors.

WHAT YOU NEED

Tools
✔ Awl
✔ Electric drill
✔ Hole saw
✔ Drill guide
✔ Utility knife
✔ Wood chisel
✔ Screwdriver

Materials
✔ Deadbolt lockset
✔ Masking tape

✋ SAFETY FIRST

Wear safety goggles when operating an electric drill.

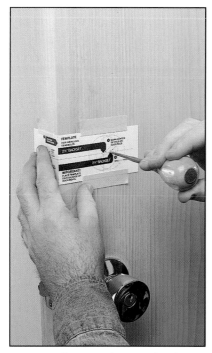

1 **Tape the template** to the door at least 6 inches above the knob. Mark the drilling locations that are appropriate for the thickness of the door with an awl *(above)*.

2 **With the door shut,** bore the cylinder hole with a hole saw. To prevent splintering, stop drilling as the saw's pilot bit exits. Complete the hole from the other side of the door *(above)*.

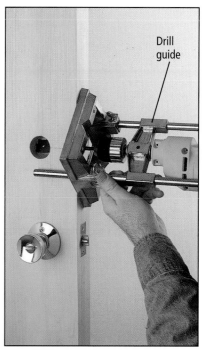

Drill guide

3 **Wedge the door open** and bore the bolt hole using a spade bit *(above)*. To ensure that the hole will be perfectly aligned, fit the drill first with a guide, as shown here.

4 **Insert the bolt assembly** and outline its faceplate on the edge of the door with a utility knife. Chisel a mortise inside the outline to match the thickness of the faceplate, then screw the assembly to the door *(above)*.

5 **Mount the cylinder assembly** on the door's exterior, sliding the drive bar through its slot in the bolt assembly. Screw the thumbturn into place on the door's interior *(above)*.

6 **Coat the bolt end** with lipstick, close the door and turn the bolt against the jamb. Bore and chisel a hole for the bolt at the mark, then chisel a mortise for the strike plate *(above)*. Screw the strike plate to the jamb.

OUTDOOR

STRUCTURES AND LANDSCAPING

PROJECT		*PAGE*
42	Staining Outdoor Structures	146
43	Framing a Ground-level Deck	150
44	Laying Deck Flooring	156
45	Putting Up a Deck Railing	160
46	Repairing Deck Posts	162
47	Building a Board-on-board Fence	164
48	Enclosing a Porch with Screens	168
49	Laying Sand-bed Brick Paving	172
50	Building a Deck Bench	178
51	Starting a Lawn	182
52	Controlling Ground Water Runoff	188

42 Staining Outdoor Structures

§💲 Estimated Savings: $1.80 per sq. foot

BEFORE YOU START

Why use stain instead of paint?

◆ Stain requires less maintenance than paint because it is less liable to chip, crack or peel. (Water-based stains, especially, stretch or compress as the wood changes density with humidity.)

◆ Stain penetrates wood with its preservatives to seal out moisture. Paint seals the wood with a waterproof coating. Wherever the coating fails water can invade the wood, collect there, and cause mildew or rot.

◆ The color is in the wood rather than on it. Latex (water-based) stain does not fade as fast as oil-based stain but neither one will need a new coat sooner than paint to preserve the color.

◆ When stain does need another coat (about 12 years after a 2-coat application) it requires less preparation than cracked, chipped or flaking paint does.

◆ Modern stains can be mixed in almost any color that paint can. The new, solid-color stains will hide differences in the color of the natural, or previously painted, wood just as well as paint does.

◆ Because stain soaks its color into the surface, rather than coats it, stain makes a more uniform color than paint on the kind of rough-finished wood usually used for barns and sheds, fences, garden furniture, and other outdoor structures.

◆ Exterior stains often contain chemical preservatives to prevent water penetration and retard mildew or rot. Some "shiny" woods, such as cedar, redwood and teak, naturally resist water but they must be weathered before staining.

◆ Though latex stain holds its texture and color better if a sealing primer is first applied over previously painted wood, it can be applied directly over a seasoned oil stain. But a sealer must be applied for an oil-based stain applied over old latex.

WHAT YOU NEED

Tools
- ✔ Stain brush
- ✔ Wire brush and scraper

Materials
- ✔ Stains and sealer

🤚 SAFETY FIRST

Protect eyes against paint splatters by covering the lid of the paint can before hammering it closed.

UNFINISHED NATURAL WOOD WITH KNOTS

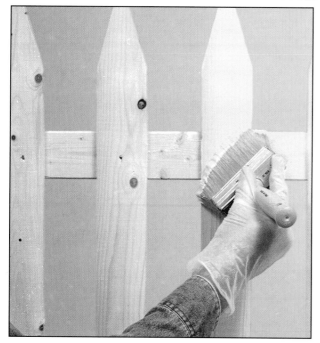

1 **Apply a primer to seal new wood with knots** or the pitch in them will soon bleed through. (Any natural wood that appears shiny needs to weather about 2 months before staining so the wood will be able to absorb the stain.)

2 **Tint the primer coat,** if necessary, to coordinate with the color of semi-transparent stains *(above),* because semi-transparent stains will reveal whatever color or blemishes exist on the wood.

A GOOD BRUSH FOR STAINING

Staining brushes have thick rows of bristles that are cut off square to carry the maximum amount of stain in one load. Pass the loaded brush over the same area only twice so you will not remove the stain before it soaks in. It is not necessary to smooth out brush strokes as it is with paints. Labels may suggest rollers or spray but professionals prefer brushes.

SOLID-COLOR VS. SEMI-TRANSPARENT

One coat of opaque, white stain (top, right) covers the natural color and patterns of the wood. A coat of a semi-transparent, oyster-grey stain (top, left) tints the wood a uniform grey tone, but does not hide its natural patterns. A clear preservative stain (bottom row) will slightly darken the wood, but provides no uniformity of tone and reveals all the wood's natural patterns.

STAINING ROUGH SIDING AND TRIM

1 Protect your landscaping with plastic sheeting or drop cloths. Drip and splatter is common because a stain brush is loaded full, and transparent stains may be thin.

2 Apply two coats to trim, especially if it is full-dimensional, rough-cut lumber *(above)*. A second coat will more than double the time before restaining is needed.

3 Use solid-color stains over new clapboard or shingle siding for an even color. The color tones of individual boards usually vary (above). The rough side of cedar siding is often exposed on outbuildings to create a rustic look. Expose cedar to the weather for 2 months before staining.

THE CLEAR STAIN ALTERNATIVE

Colorless penetrating stain preserves the wood and provides protection against soiling or mildew while retaining the wood's natural textures and patterns. A traditional preservative *(above)* is made of 1 part turpentine to 3 parts boiled linseed oil, which slightly darkens the grain of most woods. Commercial clear preservatives, available at paint dealers, can be tinted.

When to use an undercoat. Apply a sealing undercoat *(above)* when using a solid stain over an old damaged finish to prevent bleed-through or, when using a semi-transparent stain, to cover a mottled, weathered surface that would otherwise show through it.

Preparing badly weathered surfaces. Scrape and wash old paint or stain. Stain needs a clean, porous surface to penetrate; it cannot "glue" loose paint or old stain to new stain. Use a putty knife or scraping tool to clear off any loose chips of old paint, paint sags or encrusted grime. To clear loose coatings from large surfaces fit a nylon disk to an electric drill and scour weathered coatings down to a solid base. Follow up with a wire brush to loosen any remaining paint, clean rust from metal and lighten rust streaks from nails *(above)*. Touch up metal with a rust-proof primer. Mildew will bloom under stain and creep through it. To remove mildew mix 1 part bleach with 4 parts water. (To prevent toxic splashes, pour the bleach into the water, not the water into the bleach.) Wear rubber gloves and sponge the mildewed wood with the solution. Let it soak about 30 minutes to kill the mildew spores. When the surface is leveled and cleaned, rinse it with clear water while rubbing residues *(above)*. The wood must be absolutely dry to accept oil-based stains.

One-coat, solid stain over "artificial" wood. You can apply a solid-color stain, without priming, to completely cover unfinished wood products such as plywood or " T-111" siding *(above)* commonly used for barns and other outbuildings. A solid stain, especially a dark color, can completely cover plywood patches or artificial grains in one coat.

43 Framing a Ground-level Deck

💲 Estimated Savings: $560

BEFORE YOU START

◆ Sketch a detailed plan of the deck showing all dimensions to verify that the design conforms to local codes. Submission of the plan may be necessary to obtain a building permit.

◆ How the decking will be laid is a factor in deciding on the spacing of joists. Decking may be run perpendicularly across joists that are spaced 16 inches apart, but calls for a spacing of 12 inches if set diagonally.

Determining Spans

Use the charts below to select a size of joist and beam. The permissible extension of joists beyond beams and beams beyond posts is $\frac{1}{3}$ the length of the spans given. With this information, the number and spacing of posts necessary can be calculated.

Ribbon board — Joist — Bridging — Post — Footing — Beam

MAXIMUM JOIST SPAN

Joist Size	Joist Spacing	
	12"	16"
2x6	11'7"	9'9"
2x8	15'0"	12'10"
2x10	19'6"	16'5"

MAXIMUM BEAM SPAN

Beam Size	Joist Span			
	6'	8'	10'	12'
2x6 (2)	8'	7'	6'	5'
2x8 (2)	10'	9'	8'	7'
2x10 (2)	12'	11'	10'	9'
2x12 (2)	14'	13'	12'	11'

✋ SAFETY FIRST

Locate underground utilities before digging postholes. Wear safety goggles when using a circular saw and an electric drill. Wear a dust mask to cut lumber.

WHAT YOU NEED

Tools
- ✔ Tape measure
- ✔ Claw hammer
- ✔ Carpenter's square
- ✔ Plumb bob
- ✔ Posthole digger
- ✔ Mortar tub

- ✔ Shovel
- ✔ Hacksaw
- ✔ Carpenter's level
- ✔ Trowel
- ✔ Water level
- ✔ Circular saw
- ✔ Electric drill

Materials
- ✔ Mason's cord
- ✔ Chalk
- ✔ 2-by-2 stakes
- ✔ 1-by-2 braces
- ✔ Nails
- ✔ Concrete mix

- ✔ 8-inch cylindrical forms
- ✔ 4-by-4 posts
- ✔ 2-by-6 or larger beams, joists and bridging
- ✔ Framing connectors
- ✔ Exterior screws (or nails)

POSTS AND BEAMS

 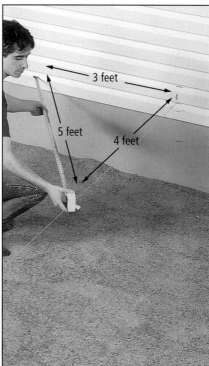

1 **To each of two stakes,** tie a length of mason's cord 2 feet longer than the width of the deck, then mark inside-corner post locations on the wall with nails. At each nail, use a carpenter's square as a guide to extend a cord at a 90° angle to the wall *(above, left)*. Check for square with a 3-4-5 triangle *(above, right)*, moving each stake as needed so that a mark on the cord 4 feet from the wall meets the 5-foot mark on a tape measure.

2 **Establish outside-corner post** locations by first marking the cords where the outer face of each outside-corner post will lie. Stake cords perpendicularly across the marks, then use a plumb bob and chalk to mark the ground where the cords intersect *(above)*.

Posthole digger

3 Dig holes for footings at the chalk marks 12 inches in diameter *(above, left)* and 8 inches below the frost line— no less than 24 inches deep. (If the cords interfere with digging, remove them from the stakes temporarily.) Enlarge each

hole at the bottom to a diameter of 16 inches, then shovel in an 8-inch base of concrete *(above, right)* and let it set for at least 24 hours.

Trowel

4 Cut cylindrical forms at least 1 inch longer than the depth of the holes with a hacksaw. Insert the forms into the holes and position each post, bracing adjacent sides and checking for plumb with a carpenter's level *(above, left)*. Pack

soil around each form and fill it with concrete, sloping the top away from the post *(above, right)* so that water will run off. Wait at least 24 hours, then remove the braces and trim the forms to below ground level.

HEIGHTS
------- Decking
------- Joist

------- Beam

------- Post

5 **Mark the decking height** on the wall, then measure off distances equal to the depth of decking, joists and beams to find the height of the posts *(inset)*. Mark each post at the correct height using a water level *(above, left)*. To trim the posts, cut across each face with a circular saw set to a cutting depth of 2 inches *(above, right)*; nail a straightedged board to the post, as shown, as a saw guide.

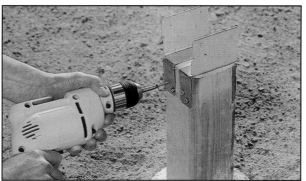

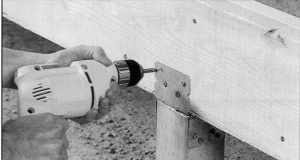

6 **Cut pairs of boards** for each beam and fasten them together from both sides at intervals of 8 inches with staggered rows of screws. Bevel the bottom ends of each beam by cutting along a diagonal line *(above, left)* drawn between marks 2 inches from the corner. Fasten post-and-beam connectors onto the tops of the posts *(above right, top)*, then mount the beams in the connectors and secure them *(above right, bottom)*.

JOISTS AND BRIDGING

End joist

Ribbon board

1 **Cut ribbon boards** and joists to length. Fasten the ribbon boards to end joists, then set the frame on the beams $\frac{1}{2}$ inch from the wall. Check that the frame is square by measuring across its diagonals *(left)*.

2 **Adjust the frame** on the beams until the distance between opposite corners is equal. Then, secure each corner of the frame and fasten the end joists to the beams with framing connectors *(left)*.

3 **Mark joist locations** on the ribbon boards, starting at the same end joist. Extend each mark onto the face of the boards *(left)* and make an X where the joist will lie.

4 **At each joist location** on the ribbon boards, position a joist hanger so that its opening is aligned at the mark and flush with the bottom. Fasten the aligned end of the hanger to the ribbon board *(left)*.

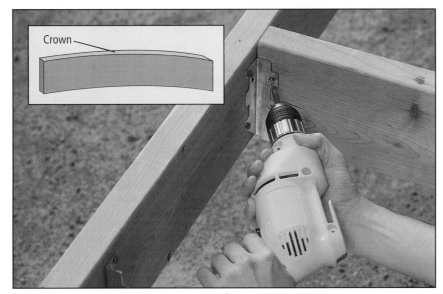

Crown

5 **Slide joists** into the hangers—being sure to position any joist that is curved along its length crown up *(inset)*. Force each hanger closed, then fasten the open end to the ribbon board and each side to the joist *(left)*.

6 **Reinforce the end joists** with bridging to support railing posts. Offset the bridging at least 4 inches from the location of a railing post and drive two fasteners into each end through the joists *(left)*.

44 Laying Deck Flooring
$ Estimated Savings: $280

BEFORE YOU START

◆ Decking of redwood or cedar will resist rot naturally, but pressure-treated pine is usually a less expensive option. Factory-machined boards 1 inch thick with rounded edges are a practical—as well as an attractive—substitute to conventional 2-by-6s or 2-by-4s.

◆ Select decking board by board, if possible. Avoid twisted or crooked stock. Boards with vertical grain—parallel grain lines along the length—often cost more, but are least likely to cup; lay a slightly cupped board convex side up to shed water.

◆ Across joists spaced 16 inches apart, decking must be laid perpendicularly. To lay decking diagonally across joists, a spacing of 12 inches is required.

◆ Butt the ends of boards that are too short to span an entire row at the center of a joist. Stagger butt joints from one row to the next so that they fall at different joists.

Decking at Opposite Diagonals

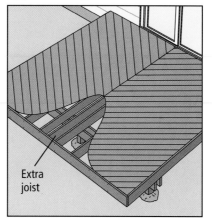

Extra joist

When laying rows of decking at opposite diagonals, an extra joist may be needed to provide a fastening surface for the ends of boards at the middle of the deck frame *(above)*. Trim rows at the centerline of the middle joist before fastening the ends of boards to it.

WHAT YOU NEED

Tools
- ✔ Tape measure
- ✔ Circular saw
- ✔ Electric drill
- ✔ Chalk line

Materials
- ✔ Decking boards
- ✔ Exterior screws (or nails)
- ✔ 2-by-6 or larger face boards

SAFETY FIRST

Wear safety goggles and a dust mask when using a circular saw.

PERPENDICULARLY ACROSS JOISTS

1 **Cut the first row** of decking to length and place it $\frac{1}{8}$ inch from the wall. Drive two screws through the decking at each joist *(above)*.

2 **Fasten subsequent rows** $\frac{1}{8}$ inch apart *(above, top)*, one end flush with an edge of the deck frame. Set the convex edge of a bowed board against the preceding row and screw one end at the usual spacing, then push the board against $\frac{1}{8}$-inch spacers at joists and secure the rest of it *(above, bottom)*.

3 **Adjust the spacing** of rows for the final 3 feet so that the last row sits flush with the edge of the deck frame *(above)*; or, rip boards of the last row by up to $\frac{1}{4}$ of their width.

4 **Using the precut end** of the first row and the face of the end joist as references, snap a chalk line across the boards extending beyond the edge of the deck frame *(above)*.

5 **Tack a straight board** to the decking as a saw guide, then trim off the ends of the overhanging boards along the line with a circular saw *(above)*.

6 **Add face boards,** if desired, for appearance. Bevel the ends of the boards to form miter joints at the corners, then mount them at the perimeter of the deck frame *(above)*.

DIAGONALLY ACROSS JOISTS

Ribbon board

End joist

1 **Mark off equal distances** from an outside corner onto the ribbon board and the end joist, then position a board at the marks and fasten it *(above)*. Lay subsequent rows on each side of the first board with a $\frac{1}{8}$-inch gap. Cut boards of the same row to meet at the center of a joist.

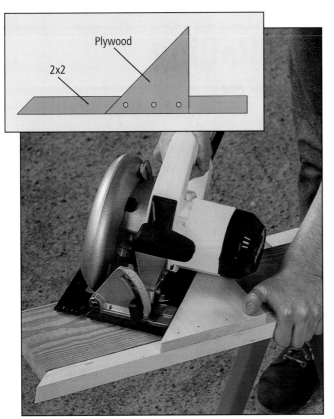

2 **Precut boards** that will lie against or within 1 foot of the wall at a 45° angle using a jig *(above)*. Make the jig out of a square of plywood with a 10-inch factory-cut edge and a straight 2-by-2 a couple of feet long *(inset)*.

3 **If laying rows** of decking at opposite diagonals—as is the case here—precut both ends of boards to fit at the inside corner. Drive fasteners at an angle into trimmed ends of boards that fall at the center of a joist *(above)*.

4 **Trim the rows** of the first diagonal at the center of the middle joist with a circular saw *(above)*, using a straight board as a saw guide. Then, fasten the trimmed ends of the boards to the middle joist.

5 **Lay out rows** of the second diagonal, precutting one end of boards abutting the first—both ends of boards against or within 1 foot of the wall. Trim the rows of both diagonals flush with the outer edges of the frame *(above)*.

45 Putting Up a Deck Railing
💲 Estimated Savings: $280

Cap rail

Picket

Post

Side rails

Railing Dimensions

A

C

B

Bridging

BEFORE YOU START

On a deck that stands at a height of 24 inches or more above ground level, a railing is usually mandatory for safety. Check local building codes for exact railing requirements and specifications:

◆ **A** Locate posts at intervals of no more than 6 feet; to reinforce the deck frame, adding bridging between joists at the perimeter may be necessary.

◆ **B** A height of 34 inches is minimum for the cap rail; if higher than 42 inches, add a middle side rail.

◆ **C** Space pickets uniformly from 2 to 6 inches apart.

WHAT YOU NEED

Tools
✔ Tape measure
✔ Circular saw
✔ Carpenter's level
✔ Electric drill

✔ Socket wrench
Materials
✔ 4-by-4 posts
✔ 2-by-4 side rails
✔ 2-by-6 cap rail

✔ 2-by-2 pickets
✔ Carriage bolts
✔ Exterior screws (or nails)

SAFETY FIRST

Wear safety goggles when drilling holes and using a circular saw. Wear a dust mask to cut lumber.

1 **Cut the posts** to size, then make a 45° bevel across their outer faces 2 inches from the bottom *(above)*.

2 **Support each post** in position on a 4-inch finishing nail driven halfway into its inner face at the top of the decking. Bore a hole through the post and deck frame, then install a carriage bolt and tighten it *(above, left)*. Checking that the post is plumb, bore a hole for a second carriage bolt *(above, right)*.

3 **Cut side rails** to fit along the inner faces of the posts. Fasten the lower side rail to the posts and at corners 2 inches above the decking *(above, left)*, the upper side rail flush with the top of the posts. Mount a cap rail on the top of the posts and upper side rail *(above, right)*, mitering corner joints.

4 **Fasten pickets** to the side rails flush with the bottom of the cap rail *(above)*. To ensure uniform intervals between pickets, use a 2-by-4 spacer.

46 Repairing Deck Posts
$ Estimated Savings: $60

BEFORE YOU START
The beam or joist supported by a post to be repaired must be braced securely with a screw jack:

◆ Set the jack on a level wood pad or concrete block directly below the beam or joist and within 2 feet of the post. Temporarily fasten a wood pad to the bottom of the beam or joist.

◆ Add to the reach of the jack, if necessary, by placing a 4-by-4 across it or by stacking concrete blocks under it.

◆ Raise the jack until it fits snugly against the beam or joist, supporting it in position without lifting it.

WHAT YOU NEED

Tools
- ✔ Screw jack
- ✔ Combination square
- ✔ Handsaw
- ✔ Wood chisel
- ✔ Mallet
- ✔ Trowel
- ✔ Plumb bob
- ✔ Electric drill
- ✔ C clamp
- ✔ Adjustable wrench

Materials
- ✔ 4-by-4 post
- ✔ Concrete mix
- ✔ Post anchor
- ✔ Carriage bolts
- ✔ Exterior screws (or nails)

CHECKING FOR ROT
A post suffering from rot may be split or cracked, but also may exhibit no visible sign. Press the tip of an awl firmly into the post *(right)*. If the wood is soft and gives way, crumbling instead of splintering, it is weakened by rot.

SAFETY FIRST

Wear safety goggles to operate an electric drill and when chiseling. Wear a dust mask to cut lumber.

1 **Brace the beam** or joist supported by the post with a screw jack, then cut the base of the post flush with the footing and saw off the damaged section. At the end of the standing post, cut an 8-inch half lap *(above)*. Boring holes and chiseling, cut the remaining post out of the footing to a depth of 8 inches *(inset)*.

2 **Fill the cavity** in the footing with concrete and set the pin of a post anchor into the center, aligned with the standing post *(above)*. Wait 24 hours, then mount the rest of the post anchor.

3 **Using the standing post** and the post anchor as guides, mark a replacement section of post for splicing *(above)*, then cut the half lap.

4 **Set the new post** into place and clamp the half-lap joint. Bore two offset holes through the joint, then install carriage bolts and tighten them *(above, left)*. Fasten the post anchor to the bottom of the post *(above, right)*.

47 Building a Board-on-board Fence
💲 Estimated Savings: $45 per 8 linear feet

BEFORE YOU START

◆ Situate the fence at a minimum of 6 inches from the property line. Check local building codes for specific setback requirements, as well as for height and other restrictions.

◆ Set posts at planned intervals of up to 8 feet; to avoid having to rip fencing boards to fit, add into calculations their width and spacing.

◆ For greatest privacy, space fencing boards at a uniform distance 2 or 3 inches less than their width.

◆ Pressure-treated wood resists rot and decay, but sawed ends should be sealed with a preservative. Untreated wood is less time-consuming to paint before it is mounted.

WHAT YOU NEED

Tools
- ✔ Sledgehammer
- ✔ Tape measure
- ✔ Line level
- ✔ Posthole digger
- ✔ Carpenter's level
- ✔ Claw hammer
- ✔ Shovel
- ✔ Trowel

- ✔ Chalk line
- ✔ Circular saw
- ✔ Electric drill

Materials
- ✔ Mason's cord
- ✔ 2-by-2 stakes
- ✔ 1-by-2 gauge pole and braces
- ✔ Gravel

- ✔ Nails
- ✔ 4-by-4 posts
- ✔ Concrete mix
- ✔ Hangers
- ✔ Exterior screws (or nails)
- ✔ 2-by-4 rails
- ✔ 1-by-6 fencing
- ✔ Post caps

SAFETY FIRST

Locate underground utilities before digging postholes. Wear safety goggles and a dust mask when cutting lumber.

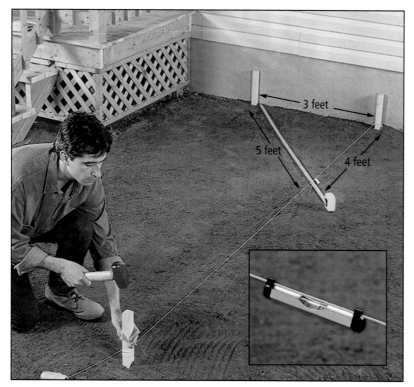

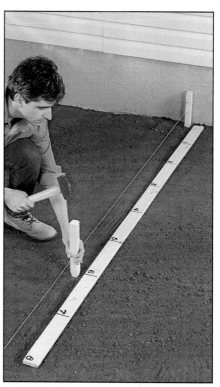

1 **Mark the fence line** with stakes and mason's cord, using a 3-4-5 triangle to check for square *(above)*. With a line level as a guide, adjust the cord until it is level *(inset)*.

2 **Space intermediate posts** using a gauge pole marked in one-foot increments, then drive a stake into the ground to mark each location *(above)*.

3 **With a posthole digger,** dig a hole for each post *(above)* 12 inches in diameter and 8 inches below the frost line—no less than 24 inches deep. Fill each hole with a 4-inch layer of gravel.

POWER AUGER

A power auger can be worthwhile if digging a large number of postholes in ground that isn't rocky. Follow the manufacturer's operating instructions carefully, raising the bit after every few inches of digging to clear out soil *(right)*.

4 **Place each end post** into its hole. Checking for plumb with a carpenter's level, tack braces to adjacent sides of the post *(above)*.

5 **Run a mason's cord** between end posts and align each intermediate post with it. Check for plumb and brace adjacent sides of the post *(above)*.

6 **Fill the hole** for each end post with concrete *(above)*. With a trowel, slope the concrete away from the post so that water will run off *(inset)*.

7 **Backfill holes** for intermediate posts, adding a 4-inch layer of soil at a time and tamping with a 2-by-4 *(above)*. Grade the soil so that water will drain away from the post.

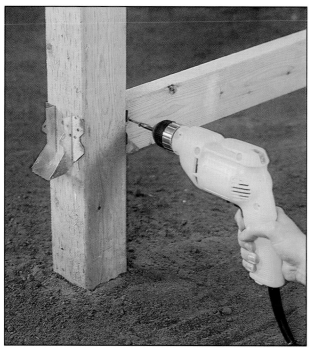

8 **Mark rail locations** on the posts with a chalk line and a line level. Mount the rails between and centered on the posts with hangers *(above)*.

Spacer

9 **Fasten fencing boards** to each side of the rails *(above)*. Hang a spacer from the top rail, as shown, to ensure that boards are placed at the same height and spaced uniformly. Check for plumb with a carpenter's level.

10 **Trim the posts** to height with a circular saw *(above)*, clamping a board in place, as shown, as a saw guide. Center a cap on the top of each post and fasten it *(inset)*.

SLOPE STEPPING

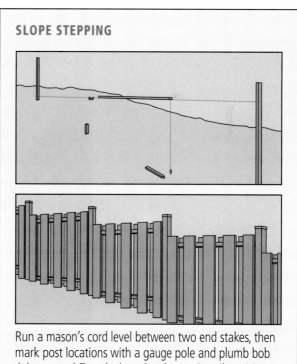

Run a mason's cord level between two end stakes, then mark post locations with a gauge pole and plumb bob *(above, top)*. To calculate the change in rail positions between posts, divide the vertical drop—height of the cord at the bottom of the slope—by the number of rail runs. Complete the fence as if the ground were level *(above, bottom)*.

48 Enclosing a Porch with Screens

💲 Estimated Savings: $280

BEFORE YOU START

◆ Plan to set framework back from the edges if the porch has round, tapered columns *(right)*. (Square, flat-surfaced posts may be used as frame corners.)

◆ Remove railings and railing posts at the perimeter of the porch.

◆ Space studs at uniform intervals of no more than 5 feet.

WHAT YOU NEED

Tools
✔ Chalk line
✔ Carpenter's square
✔ Tape measure
✔ Stepladder
✔ Plumb bob
✔ Circular saw
✔ Electric drill
✔ Carpenter's level
✔ Compass
✔ Saber saw
✔ Claw hammer
✔ Staple gun
✔ Utility knife

Materials
✔ 2-by-4s
✔ Exterior screws (or nails)
✔ 1-by-1s
✔ Finishing nails (2-inch)
✔ Screening
✔ Staples
✔ Screen door
✔ Door hinges

SAFETY FIRST

Wear safety goggles when using a power saw and driving fasteners. Wear a dust mask to cut lumber.

1 **Mark the frame location** on the floor with a chalk line, then note positions for intermediate studs *(above)* and for the doorway opening. Using a plumb bob, transfer the frame location to the ceiling.

2 **Cut 2-by-4s to length** for the sole and top plates, then fasten them to the floor and the ceiling every 16 inches *(above)*—if possible, to joists. (Leave a doorway opening in the sole plate $3\frac{1}{4}$ inches larger than the door's width.)

Sole plate
2-by-4

3 **For each corner post,** cut two 2-by-4s to fit between the sole plate and top plate. Position the 2-by-4s and check that they are plumb *(above)*, then drive fasteners at an angle *(inset)* to secure them to the sole plate and top plate.

4 **Cut end studs** to size, then transfer the siding profile onto them using a compass *(above)* and cut the profile with a saber saw. Fasten each end stud to the sole plate and top plate and at 8-inch intervals to the siding.

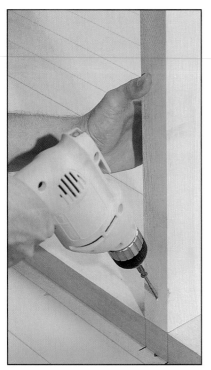

King stud

Header

Jack stud

5 **Mount intermediate studs** at the marked locations, driving fasteners at an angle into the sole plate *(above)* and top plate.

6 **Frame the doorway** with two full-height (king) studs and two door-height (jack) studs with a header, allowing $\frac{1}{4}$ inch of clearance for the door. Mount the king studs between the sole plate and top plate, then fasten the jack studs to the king studs and secure the header *(above)*.

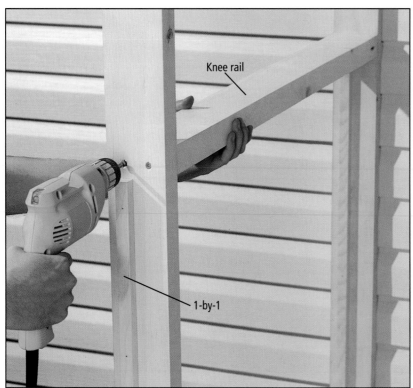

Knee rail

1-by-1

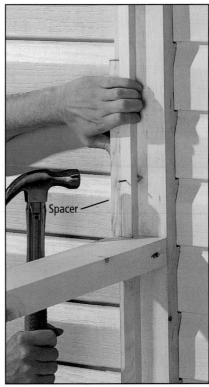

Spacer

7 **Add a knee rail** between studs 3 feet above the sole plate and frame each opening with 1-by-1 blocking. Begin by nailing 3-foot lengths of blocking onto the lower outer side of each stud's midpoint with a 1-by-1 spacer, then secure the knee rail in place *(above, left)* and complete the frame *(above, right)*.

8 **Cut pieces of screening** a few inches larger than each opening and staple them at intervals of 2 inches to the blocking *(above, left)*. Frame the interior side of each opening with 1-by-1 blocking, then trim off excess screening with a utility knife *(above, right)*.

PREFRAMED SCREENS

Frame each opening with stops set back from the exterior by a distance equal to the thickness of the screen frame *(below)*. Then, fasten a pair of turn buttons to both sides of each opening to hold the screen frame against the stops *(inset)*.

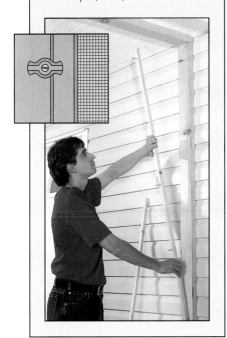

9 **Screw hinges** to the outside of the door 12 inches from the top and bottom. Using wood scraps as a foot lever to prop the door in position, mark the location of screw holes *(above, left)*, then bore pilot holes and screw in the hinges. With a spacer equal to the door's thickness, nail stops to the frame *(above, right)*.

171

49 Laying Sand-bed Brick Paving

$ Estimated Savings: $50 per 100 sq. ft.

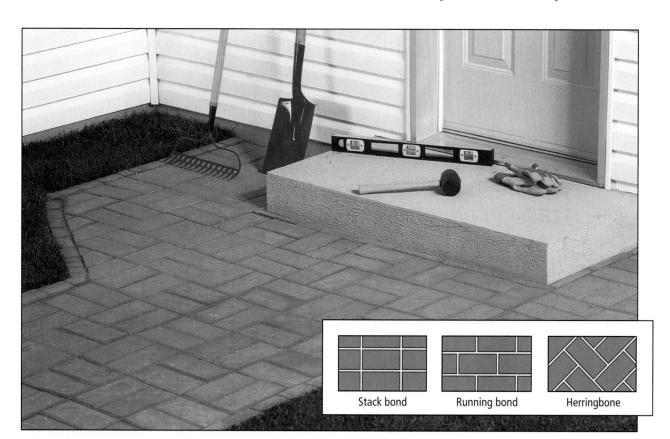

Stack bond   Running bond   Herringbone

BEFORE YOU START

◆ Paving bricks and paving of molded concrete are available in a wide variety of colors, sizes and shapes; interlocking paving *(right)* is least likely to shift after installation.

◆ For rectangular paving bricks, choose a basket-weave *(above)* or other classic pattern *(inset)* — or combine patterns.
◆ To avoid having to cut a large number of paving bricks, lay out a dry run and adjust dimensions to accommodate as many whole bricks as possible.

SAFETY FIRST

Locate underground utilities before excavating. Wear safety goggles to cut bricks and a dust mask when operating a circular saw.

WHAT YOU NEED

Tools
✔ Tape measure
✔ Small sledgehammer
✔ Carpenter's square
✔ T-bevel
✔ Protractor
✔ Garden spade

✔ Wheelbarrow
✔ Tamper
✔ Line level
✔ Shovel
✔ Garden rake
✔ Utility knife
✔ Screed

✔ Rubber mallet
✔ Carpenter's level
✔ Brickset and maul
✔ Circular saw and mason's hammer
✔ Garden hose
✔ Broom

Materials
✔ Mason's cord
✔ 2-by-2 stakes
✔ Gravel (washed ¾-inch)
✔ Landscaping fabric
✔ Sand
✔ Brick pavers

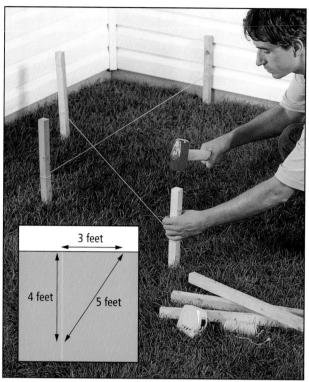

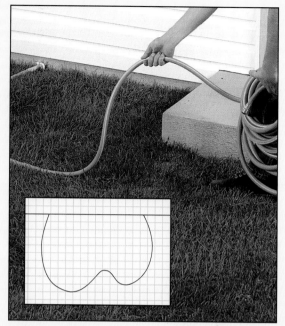

3 feet

4 feet

5 feet

1 **Mark off the perimeter** with stakes and mason's cord *(above)*, using a 3-4-5 triangle to form corners at a 90° angle *(inset)*. Check corners at other angles with a T-bevel and a protractor.

Draw the shape to scale on graph paper *(inset)*, with each square representing 1 square foot. Then, transfer the plan to the site with a garden hose *(above)* and mark the outline with chalk.

2 **Excavate the site** to a depth of 8 to 10 inches *(above, left)*—enough to accommodate gravel, sand and bricks. Compact the surface with a tamper *(above, right)* made out of a 2-foot square of ¾-inch plywood and a braced 4-foot length of 2-by-4 with handles.

3 **Dig a narrow trench** at the perimeter of the site deep enough to stand bricks on end as edging *(above)*. Tamp the soil in the bottom of the trench with the end of a 2-by-4.

4 **Adjust the height** of the cords on the stakes to the level of the edging, checking with a line level *(above)*.

5 **Set edging bricks** in the trench using the cords to align them *(above)*. Check for level with a carpenter's level and backfill soil around the bricks to hold them in place.

EDGING ALTERNATIVES

Options include pressure-treated lumber *(right, top)* and inter-locking edging of concrete *(right, bottom)*. Bricks can be placed at an angle to make a sawtooth pattern *(below)*.

6 **For drainage,** add a 3- to 4-inch layer of gravel *(above)*. Compact the gravel with a tamper.

7 **Apply landscaping fabric** to inhibit growth of weeds *(above)*. (Polyethylene sheeting or other similar material may be used if it is punctured with drainage holes at 4- to 6-inch intervals.)

8 **Cover the fabric** with 3 to 4 inches of sand *(above)*— enough so that bricks will sit flush with the edging. Mist the sand using a garden hose, then compact it with a tamper.

9 **Smooth and level** the sand using a straight length of 2-by-4 as a screed *(above)*. Fill in low spots with sand and tamp them.

10 **Place bricks** of the first row, tapping each one with a rubber mallet to seat it flush *(above)*. Check that bricks are level with a carpenter's level.

11 **Align bricks** of subsequent rows using a reference cord wrapped around bricks set against the outside edge of opposite edging bricks *(above)*.

POWER PAVING CUTTER

A power paving cutter can be worthwhile if there are a large number of bricks to cut or bricks must be cut precisely at beveled or other special angles *(right)*. While operating the cutter, wear safety goggles, hearing protection and a dust mask and make sure that the blade is kept cool by a constant flow of water.

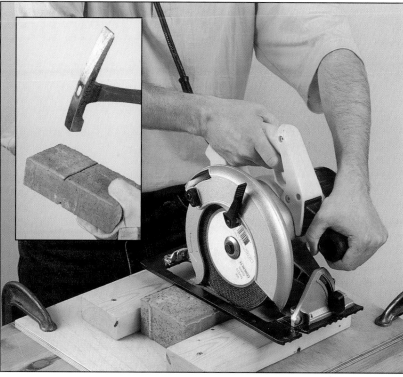

12 **Cut bricks** with a brickset and a maul, alternately tilting slightly into and against the cut and striking sharply *(above, left)*. Or, using a jig made of plywood and 2-by-4s, saw a $\frac{1}{4}$-inch groove in the top and bottom of each brick with a carbide-tipped blade *(above, right)*, then snap off the waste with a mason's hammer *(inset)*.

13 **When all the bricks** have been placed, spread a fine layer of sand on them. Dampen the sand and sweep it into the spaces between bricks *(above)*. Add more sand, if necessary, after the first heavy rain.

CIRCLE-BASED PAVING

Curved Surrounds
Set edging bricks at the inner perimeter in an arc at least 3 feet in diameter to avoid large gaps between bricks. Lay two rows of half bricks *(left)*, then continue with rows of whole bricks. Cut bricks as necessary to fit gaps along edging bricks at the outer perimeter.

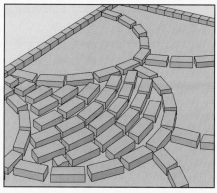

Overlapping Arcs
Place edging bricks, then outline arcs with whole bricks—arcs with a radius of 24 inches and centers spaced 60 inches apart make an attractive pattern. Within each full and partial arc, lay curving rows of whole bricks and fill in gaps with cut bricks *(left)*.

50 Building a Deck Bench
💲 Estimated Savings: $280

Side rail

Cap rail

Seating plank

Seating support

Trim

Post

BEFORE YOU START

Check local building codes for specific requirements on deck benches:

◆ Locate posts at joists or bridging no more than 6 feet apart.

◆ Leave a uniform gap between side rails of from 2 to 6 inches.

◆ Place seating supports at intervals no greater than 30 inches and within 18 inches of corners.

WHAT YOU NEED

Tools
- ✔ Carpenter's square
- ✔ Electric drill
- ✔ Saber saw
- ✔ Carpenter's protractor
- ✔ Adjustable wrench
- ✔ Clamp

- ✔ Circular saw
- ✔ T-bevel
- ✔ Claw hammer

Materials
- ✔ 4-by-4 posts
- ✔ Bridging
- ✔ 2-by-6 side rails, cap rail and seat planks

- ✔ 2-by-10 seat supports
- ✔ 1-by-2 trim
- ✔ Carriage bolts
- ✔ Exterior screws (or nails)
- ✔ Finishing nails

✋ SAFETY FIRST

Wear safety goggles when drilling holes and using a circular saw. Wear a dust mask to cut lumber.

BACKREST POST AND RAILS

1 Mark post openings of $3\frac{3}{4}$ inches by $3\frac{7}{8}$ inches on the decking, the shorter dimension parallel and $1\frac{1}{4}$ inch from its edge *(above, left)*. Through the corners of each outline, bore holes at a 15° angle away from the deck perimeter. Cut

the longer sides of the outlines with a saber saw set to cut at 90° *(above, right)*; for the shorter sides, set it to cut at a 15° angle away from the deck perimeter.

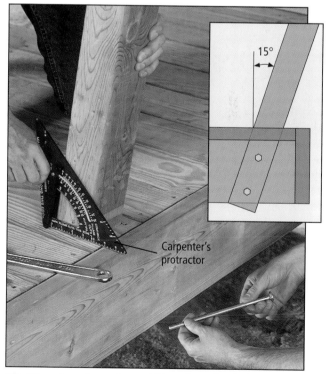

Carpenter's protractor

2 Add bridging of the same thickness and width as the joists on one longer side of each opening along the end joists *(above)*. Secure the bridging by driving fasteners into each end of it through the joists *(inset)*.

3 Mount each post at a 15° angle to the deck perimeter, aligning its inner corner with the bottom of the adjacent bridging or joist *(inset)*. Bore two holes through the post and bridging or joist, then install carriage bolts *(above)*.

First rail

4 **Measure a distance** of 36 inches from the decking on the inner face of each post and mark horizontal cutting lines across the adjacent sides. Trim the top of each post level with a circular saw *(above)*, clamping a board in place, as shown, as a saw guide.

5 **To mark side rails** at corners, prop them on nails driven halfway into the posts. Trim the end of the first rail at a $14\frac{1}{2}°$ angle and butt it against the second rail, then draw the angle of its inner face onto the second rail *(above)*.

6 **For mitered corners,** cut the ends of the side rails with a circular saw set at a 44° angle *(above)*. Fasten the rails to the posts and at corners, spacing them vertically at intervals of no more than 4 inches.

7 **Mount a cap rail** on the top of the posts and upper side rail *(above)*, mitering the ends of boards at corners at a 45° angle, as shown.

SEATING SUPPORTS AND PLANKS

 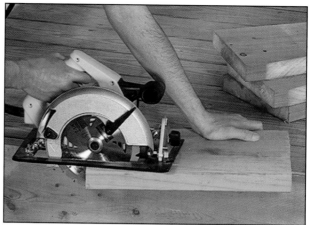

1 **Cut seating supports** 17 inches in height, then measure the angle between the decking and lower side rail with a T-bevel *(above, left)*. Trim one support at this angle with a circular saw, then use it as a template to cut the other supports *(above, right)*.

2 **Space seating supports** no more than 30 inches apart, fastening them at the bottom to the decking *(above)* and at the top to a siderail.

3 **Nail trim pieces** along the bottom edges of each seating support *(above)*.

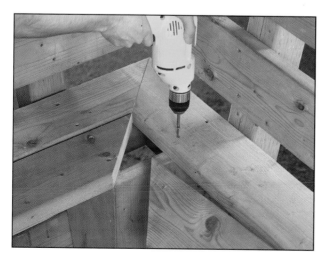

4 **Miter the ends** of seating planks at a 45° angle and mount them on the supports *(above)*, leaving a gap of $\frac{1}{8}$ inch between rows.

HERRINGBONE SEATING PLANKS

For herringbone corners, leave the ends of seating planks square and butt them end to edge *(above)*.

51 Starting a Lawn

💲 Estimated Savings: $25 per 100 sq. ft.

BEFORE YOU START

◆ Choose a planting method that is appropriate to the type of grass to be grown and how quickly the lawn needs to be established.

◆ To prepare the site for a lawn, till the soil, then rake out stones and other debris. Add peat moss, manure and other amendments as needed and

work them in thoroughly. Slope ground away from the house for drainage. Firm the soil using a half-filled roller and fill in low spots.

WHAT YOU NEED

SEED	SPRIGS	PLUGS	SOD
Tools	**Tools**	**Tools**	**Tools**
✔ Spreader	✔ Garden hose	✔ Grass plugger	✔ Garden hose
✔ Grass rake	✔ Garden hoe	✔ Garden hose	✔ Sharp knife
✔ Lawn roller	**Materials**	✔ Garden rake	✔ Lawn roller
✔ Garden hose	✔ Sprigs	**Materials**	**Materials**
Materials		✔ Plugs	✔ Sod
✔ Seed			

SOWING SEED

1 **Load seed** into a spreader and calibrate it, then make parallel, slightly overlapping passes back and forth from one end of the site to the other. Walk at a moderate pace behind the spreader and close it at the end of each row *(above, left)* to reposition it. Make a second series of passes *(above, right)* at a 90° angle to the first rows.

2 **Rake the area** lightly to mix the seed thoroughly into the soil *(above, top)*, then roll it with a half-filled roller to embed the seed in the soil *(above, bottom)*.

3 **Mist with water** from a garden hose *(above)*—enough to keep the area moist without forming puddles. Water at least once daily until seedlings reach a height of $\frac{1}{2}$ inch.

PLANTING SPRIGS

1 Mist the soil with water *(above)*, soaking it thoroughly. Allow the water to seep into the soil for 24 hours.

2 With a garden hoe, cut a series of straight furrows 3 to 4 inches deep and 6 to 12 inches apart *(above)*.

3 Place sprigs into each furrow at 6- to 12-inch intervals, slanting them upward from the bottom to the top of one side *(above, left)*. Press soil around the roots, leaving some blades of each sprig protruding *(above, right)*. Mist with water as necessary to keep the soil moist until the sprigs take root.

PLANTING PLUGS

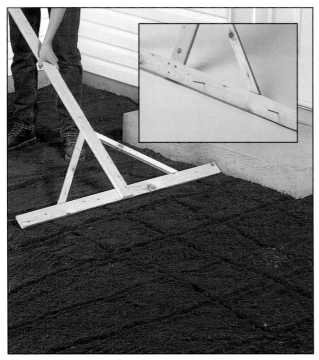

1 **Soak the soil,** then let the water seep in for 24 hours. Mark locations for plugs at intervals of 12 to 18 inches with a spacing tool *(inset)*, dragging it across the area in two series of parallel passes at a 90° angle to each other *(above, left)*. At each intersection of scratched lines, dig a hole with a grass plugger *(above, right)*.

2 **Fill each hole** with water *(above, top)* and let it drain. Insert a plug in the hole *(above, bottom)* and step gently on it to press it into place level with the surrounding soil.

3 **Break up cores** of extracted soil and lightly smooth the ground between plugs *(above)*. Water daily for 2 weeks, then every other day for a month until the plugs take root.

LAYING SOD

1 **Soak the soil** and allow the water to seep in for at least 24 hours. Mist lightly to moisten the soil again just before laying the sod *(above)*.

2 **Lay the first course** of sod along a straight reference edge *(above)* or using stakes and mason's cord. Unroll the sod gently to avoid breaking off corners and edges.

3 **Unroll the sod** for subsequent courses, butting edges together as tightly as possible *(above)* and staggering joints. If the sod seems uneven, roll it up enough to level the ground under it. To avoid creating depressions in sod that is already laid, kneel on a piece of plywood or planking.

To hold rolls of sod in place on slopes, drive in 1-by-1 stakes *(above)*. Remove the stakes when the sod has taken root and fill the holes with soil.

4 Trim off excess sod at the end of courses with a sharp knife *(above)*. Use these cut pieces to fill oddly-shaped spots at the perimeter of the site.

5 Roll the sod with an empty roller to embed it in the soil *(above)*. Water the sod daily for 2 weeks—more often at the edges and other exposed places that tend to dry quickly.

6 Test the sod after 2 weeks by trying to lift it by blades of grass *(above)*. If the blades of grass tear, the sod has taken root and can be watered less frequently; otherwise, water daily for a few more days and test again.

187

52 Controlling Ground Water Runoff

💲 Estimated Savings: $120

WHAT YOU NEED

Tools
- ✔ Tape measure
- ✔ Long-handled shovel
- ✔ Posthole digger (optional)
- ✔ Hand saw
- ✔ Rake

Materials
- ✔ PVC drywell pipe, 4-inch diameter: perforated and solid, elbows, downspout adapter
- ✔ Liquid PVC cement
- ✔ Plastic sheeting
- ✔ Gravel
- ✔ Landscaping materials

✋ SAFETY FIRST

Protect back muscles when digging by bending your knees. Push shovel into earth by leaning, not jabbing.

BEFORE YOU START

◆ To prevent rainwater from seeping into your cellar or eroding your foundation, you'll need to give the ground time and space to run the water away from your foundation or absorb it downward before it accumulates.

◆ For light rainfall, sandy porous soil and no cellar to worry about, a simple splashblock at the bottom of the downspout may do.

◆ The common solution to heavy roof runoff: Gutters at the sloping ends of the roof collect runoff, then downspouts carry the water into pipes or other devices that divert it away from the foundation into a drywell pit where it can soak into the earth rapidly.

◆ If the builder did not grade the earth surrounding the foundation to carry rainwater away, it can collect and seep into the cellar. Heavy equipment and professional help may be necessary to remedy that.

◆ If your house is on an incline and water collects on the uphill side of the house, you can dig a trench between the house and the hill, fill it with gravel and route it around the house to carry the water downhill. (See "Swale & Berm," page 191.)

Gravel Guide: What size do I use for what purpose?

Use $\frac{3}{4}$-inch for drainage and drywells. Silt and debris can pass through it.

Use $\frac{1}{2}$-inch for driveways. It doesn't stick in tire treads but packs down enough to drive on.

Use $\frac{3}{8}$-inch peastone for foundation concrete mix and landscaping.

EASY DRYWELL

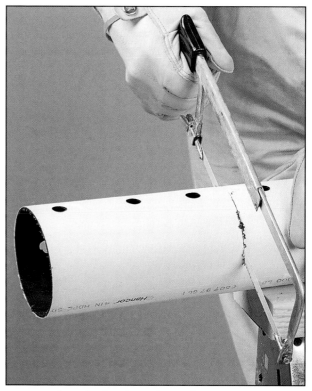

1 **Dig a 1-foot-deep trench** leading 2 to 4 feet away from the downspout and just wide enough to bury a 4-inch diameter drywell pipe. At the outer end of the trench, dig a drywell hole about 3 feet deep and 18 inches in diameter. Before you dig, clear away landscaping materials you want to save. The goal is to carry downspout water away and downhill.

2 **Cut a length** of perforated drywell pipe about 6 inches less than the depth of the drywell hole. Cut 2 lengths of unperforated 4-inch-diameter PVC drywell pipe. Cut one about 12 inches long to extend the downspout. Cut another long enough to lie in the trench. You will also need two elbows and a downspout adapter (see page 190).

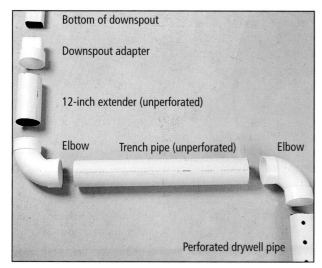

Bottom of downspout

Downspout adapter

12-inch extender (unperforated)

Elbow   Trench pipe (unperforated)   Elbow

Perforated drywell pipe

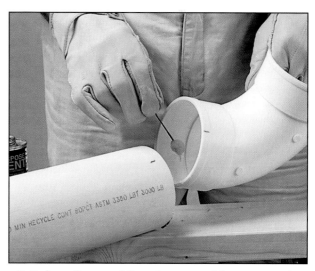

3 **Loosely assemble** pipe lengths before gluing as shown above. Fit a downspout adapter onto one end of the 12-inch extender. Add an elbow and fit it to the solid "trench" pipe. Add another elbow and fit it to the "drywell" pipe. Place the assembly into the trench and hole. Adjust lengths and angles. Be sure the adapter and gutter line up.

4 **Before disassembling,** draw a pencil line across each joint so you can line up the components correctly later. Glue assembly together by coating each face with all-purpose liquid PVC cement. Press into place with marks lined up. After the glue dries, place the assembly into the trench and down into the drywell.

5 **Shovel ¾-inch gravel** into the trench, drywell hole and around the pipe. Stop filling when the gravel in the hole and trench is even with the top of the pipe in the trench *(above)*.

6 **Cover the gravel** with sheet plastic to prevent landscaping materials from clogging the holes in the drywell pipe. Continue filling the hole and trench with sand *(above)* up to 2 inches below grade level. Sand allows water to drain into the drywell before it can pool next to the foundation.

7 **Rake the area smooth** to prepare for landscaping with mulch, shrubs, grass or floral border. Note that at least 8 inches of the cement foundation have remained above the landscaped grade as a barrier to prevent insects or vermin from invading the house.

DOWNSPOUT ADAPTERS

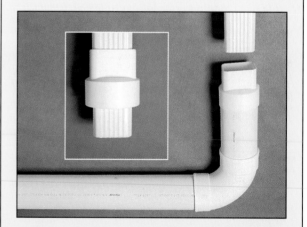

The bottom end of the downspout fits inside an adapter which then fits around the end of 4-inch PVC drywell pipe *(above, right)*. It is important that the downspout and drywell pipe are cut to the right lengths to allow the adapter to join them. If in doubt, cut the downspout a little long, because it can slide down into the adapter. If the downspout cannot be moved slide the adapter onto its end *(inset)* before you bury the pipe.

GRADING GROUND

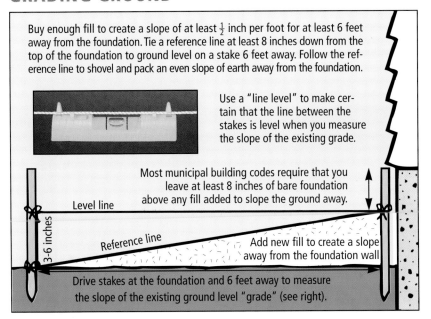

Buy enough fill to create a slope of at least $\frac{1}{2}$ inch per foot for at least 6 feet away from the foundation. Tie a reference line at least 8 inches down from the top of the foundation to ground level on a stake 6 feet away. Follow the reference line to shovel and pack an even slope of earth away from the foundation.

Use a "line level" to make certain that the line between the stakes is level when you measure the slope of the existing grade.

Most municipal building codes require that you leave at least 8 inches of bare foundation above any fill added to slope the ground away.

Level line

3-6 inches

Reference line

Add new fill to create a slope away from the foundation wall

Drive stakes at the foundation and 6 feet away to measure the slope of the existing ground level "grade" (see right).

Measure the slope away from the foundation wall. Drive a stake next to the wall and another 6 feet out from it. Tie a string next to the ground at the wall and run it to the outer stake. Hang a line level on the string and adjust the outer end to level it. If the distance between the string and the ground at the outer stake is at least 3 inches, the slope is adequate. If not, move the string up the outer stake 3 to 6 inches above the ground; then move the string at the wall up the stake until it is level. Tie a string from that point to the ground at the outer stake. Add earth "fill" following that slope away from the foundation. Leave at least 8 inches of wall bare above the fill or find another solution *(below)* to avoid excavation.

FRENCH DRAIN

Make a gravel-filled ditch along the foundation under the eaves to prevent ground water from a sloping grade or roof runoff from building up and penetrating the foundation. Position the ditch (about $1\frac{1}{2}$ feet wide and $2\frac{1}{2}$ feet deep) along the foundation on the side where the grade slopes down. Turn the ends downhill on either side to carry the water away. After filling it with gravel, insert a permanent edging where the gravel and surface earth meet to block earth, debris and vegetation from invading and clogging the gravel trench.

SWALE & BERM

If water runoff is a problem on the uphill side of the house, dig a shallow trench called a "swale" a few feet away from the foundation to divert water. It should be about 2 feet wide and 8 inches deep and run along the uphill side and around the house to lead down hill. Slope mounded earth, called "berm," from the uphill facing side of the foundation down into the trench. Compact it by watering it and pounding it with a shovel. Fill the trench with gravel to help absorb water runoff. Replace the grass to cover the mound and gravel.

TOOLS

AND TECHNIQUES

The Home Workshop 194

Personal Safety Gear 196

Measurers & Markers 198

Using Straightedges, Squares, & T-bevels 199

Hammers 203

Fastening with Screws 204

Cutters 208

Handsaws 209

Wrenches 210

Pliers & Clamps 211

Planes & Files 212

Chisels, Awls, & Punches 213

Power Tools 214

Plumber's Aids 216

General Tools 217

Dealing with Hazards 219

Dealing with Emergencies 221

The Home Workshop

Hardly any project, including the erection of an entire house, needs every tool found in a hardware store. But for basic repairs and improvements, a homeowner should have a reasonably comprehensive tool kit. This chapter is a guide for assembling a basic set of tools and safety equipment for common do-it-yourself projects.

Assembling the right tools

When it comes to choosing tools, let the job pick them for you. In this way, you buy only the items you need, when you need them. If you own just a few tools, the first project you tackle may require extensive purchases. But the second will probably mean the addition of only a few more tools, and eventually a complete set will all but assemble itself. Such a buy-as-you-go philosophy is obviously inappropriate for some items. It makes more sense to take home a complete set of wrenches or bits for a drill, for example, than to buy them separately.

Hand tools are adequate for most small projects and have obvious advantages if you are working outdoors far from electrical outlets. However, a power tool is an asset where the amount of work to be done or the precision required justifies its price. Some projects call for specialized tools that are not really part of a basic home tool kit. Included in this category are such items as floor sanders and concrete mixers. Many of these tools can be rented.

Tips on buying

Do not be tempted by cheap prices. Shoddy screwdrivers and hammers will break, possibly causing injury and damaging the work. Tools should help minimize errors, not create them.

When choosing a tool, look for the name of a reputable manufacturer. High-quality tools—because they last for years—are the only true bargains. However, it is rarely necessary to own the most expensive lines; generally they offer only subtle improvements in balance and workmanship. For the home workshop these qualities may not justify the price.

Heft the tool to test its balance, making sure that it is neither too heavy to handle nor too light to do a good job. Try to test display models of power tools to observe them in operation. Stick with double-insulated power tools; their shockproof housing will relieve you of any concern about whether electrical outlets—and the tool—are properly grounded.

Before settling on a brand or model, read the terms of the manufacturer's

guarantee. Many hand tools have unconditional, lifetime warranties that promise a replacement if the tool breaks in normal use. You should expect power tools to be guaranteed for at least a full year and to have easily replaceable parts.

Making tools work for you

Use the right tool for the job. The wrong tool often makes it impossible to achieve professional-looking results. Remember that the tools should do most of the work for you; they become inefficient and difficult to control when too much force is applied. Swing a hammer so the weight of the head—not your muscle—drives the nail. Saw without excessive pressure; if the saw is as sharp as it should be, it will cut quickly and hold to a straight line. Excessive force used with power tools can overheat motors and scatter dangerous fragments of blades and bits. Tools function safely and reliably if they are properly looked after. Clean saw-

dust, grease, and dirt from them after each use, and hang them up instead of dumping them into a toolbox, where they will be hard to find and subject to damage. Keep tools sharp. You can renew the edges of planes and chisels yourself; however, most saw blades, because of their compound bevels, and all drill and router bits require special sharpening tools and techniques that are available from professionals.

Safety precautions

To prevent accidents, keep an orderly work area that is free of clutter. Wear safety gear to protect your eyes from flying debris, your ears and lungs from the din and dust of power tools, and your hands from sharp, toxic, or abrasive materials. Wear close-fitting clothing, tie back long hair, and remove all jewelry—including rings and watches—that might be caught in the tool as you work. Use clamps to lock workpieces firmly. Follow all the instructions that come with a power tool, and

keep them for future reference.

Whenever possible, avoid using electrical tools in damp areas, even if the tools are double-insulated or grounded. Remember to disconnect power tools before changing blades or bits, and keep all adjustment nuts tight.

Personal Safety Gear

Safety goggles
Flexible, molded plastic with adjustable head-strap. Prevent eye injury from flying particles and chemical splashes.

Ear plugs
Compressible foam expands to shape of ear canal. Protect hearing against high-intensity noise.

Safety helmet
Reinforced plastic with adjustable headband. Protects head against impact injury.

Face shield
Hinged plastic guard with adjustable headstrap. Provides heavy-duty protection of eyes and face.

Ear muffs
Cushioned muffs with adjustable headstrap. Protect hearing against high-intensity noise.

Cotton gloves
For light protection in most general work situations.

Leather gloves
Heavy-duty hand protection for work with sharp or rough materials and when handling pressure-treated lumber.

Rubber gloves
Made of neoprene to prevent skin contact with finishes, solvents, strippers and adhesives.

Safety boots
Sturdy leather with steel-reinforced toes and soles protect against foot injury.

RESPIRATORY PROTECTION

Disposable dust mask
Provides single-use protection against nuisance dust or mist.

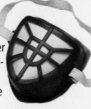

Reusable dust mask
Replaceable filter permits multiple-use protection against nuisance dust or mist.

Dual-cartridge respirator
Fitted with interchangeable filters or cartridges for protection against specific toxic dust, mist or vapor hazards.

USING A DUAL-CARTRIDGE RESPIRATOR

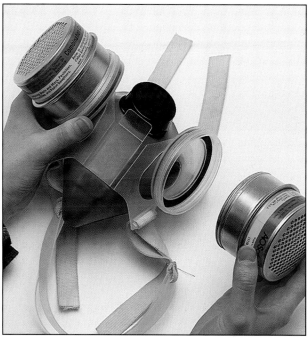

1 **Install filters or cartridges** appropriate to the protection required: filters for dust or mist; cartridges for vapor; or both for multiple hazards. Fit filters flat inside the retainers *(above, left)* and screw them to the respirator. Thread car- tridges directly into the respirator *(above, right)*. If using both filters and cartridges, first screw in the cartridges, then fit the retainers with filters and mount them onto the cartridges.

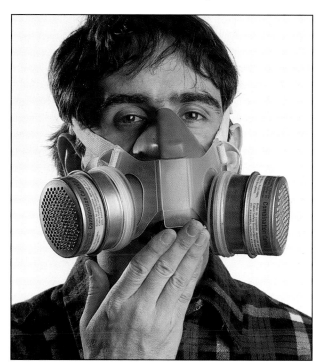

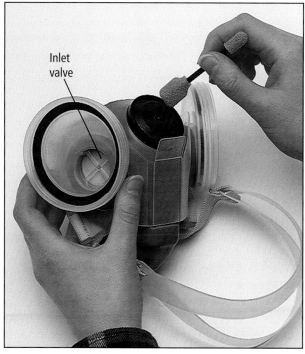

2 **Adjust the headstrap** so that the respirator fits snugly. Press the palm of your hand over the outlet valve to block it, then exhale gently *(above)*. If there is air leakage around the edges, adjust the fit of the respirator and repeat the test.

3 **After using the respirator,** disassemble it and wipe the inside and outside surfaces with a soft cloth. Use a foam swab to clean the outlet valve *(above)* and inlet valve. Check the owner's manual for special maintenance instructions. Store the respirator in a sealed plastic bag.

Measurers & Markers

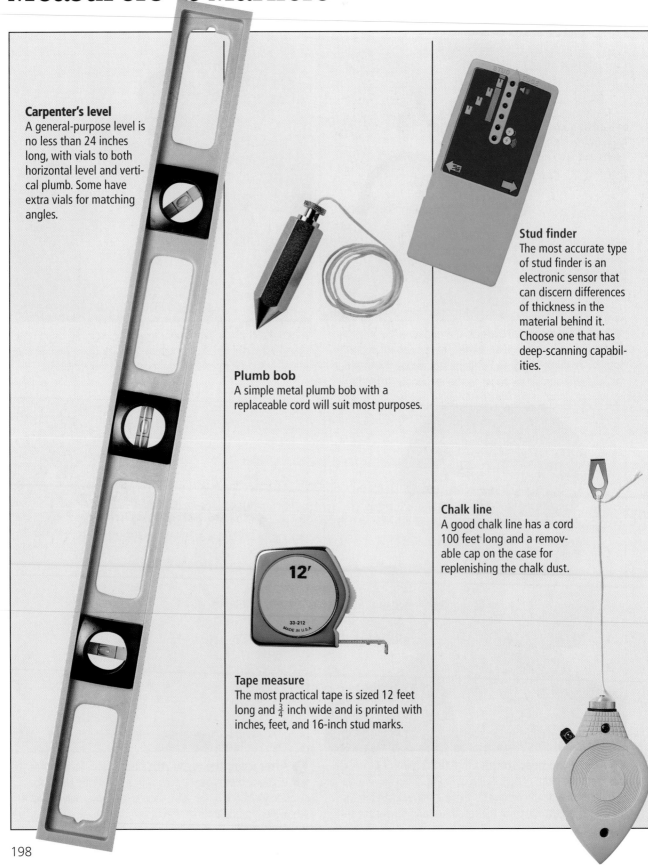

Carpenter's level
A general-purpose level is no less than 24 inches long, with vials to both horizontal level and vertical plumb. Some have extra vials for matching angles.

Stud finder
The most accurate type of stud finder is an electronic sensor that can discern differences of thickness in the material behind it. Choose one that has deep-scanning capabilities.

Plumb bob
A simple metal plumb bob with a replaceable cord will suit most purposes.

Chalk line
A good chalk line has a cord 100 feet long and a removable cap on the case for replenishing the chalk dust.

Tape measure
The most practical tape is sized 12 feet long and $\frac{3}{4}$ inch wide and is printed with inches, feet, and 16-inch stud marks.

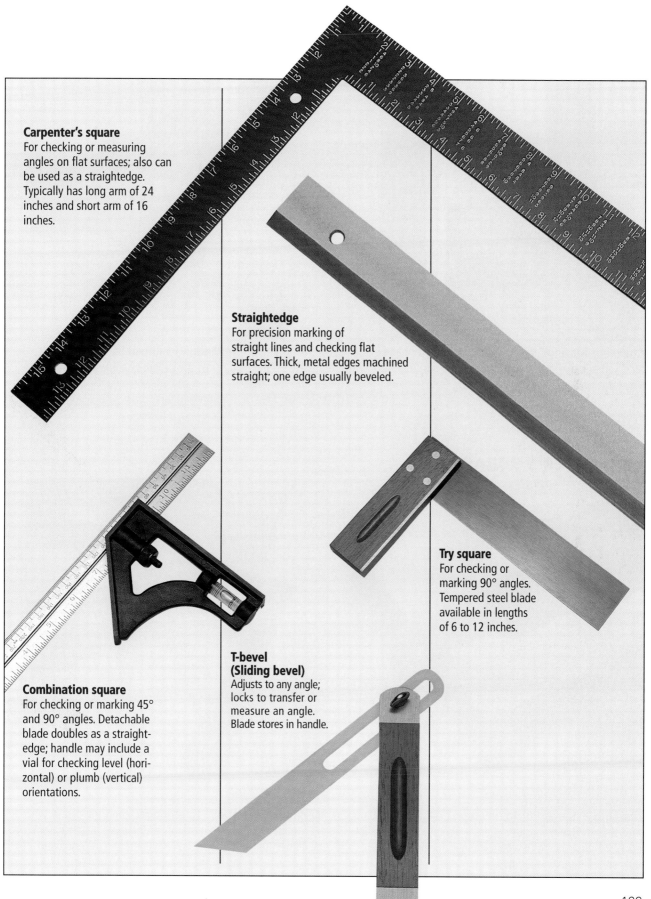

Carpenter's square
For checking or measuring angles on flat surfaces; also can be used as a straightedge. Typically has long arm of 24 inches and short arm of 16 inches.

Straightedge
For precision marking of straight lines and checking flat surfaces. Thick, metal edges machined straight; one edge usually beveled.

Try square
For checking or marking 90° angles. Tempered steel blade available in lengths of 6 to 12 inches.

Combination square
For checking or marking 45° and 90° angles. Detachable blade doubles as a straight-edge; handle may include a vial for checking level (horizontal) or plumb (vertical) orientations.

T-bevel (Sliding bevel)
Adjusts to any angle; locks to transfer or measure an angle. Blade stores in handle.

TRY SQUARE

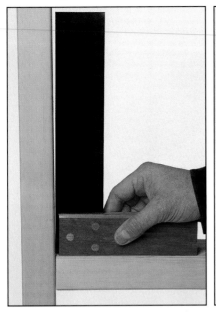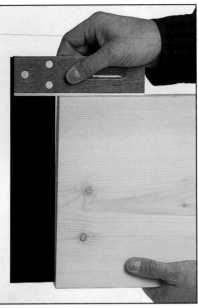

Checking for a 90° angle. Hold the square's handle against the reference surface and butt the blade against the other surface. Work with the square's outer edges to check an inside angle *(above, left)*, the inner edges for an outside angle *(above, right)*. A visible gap between the blade and the surface, as shown here, indicates an angle other than 90°.

Marking a line at 90° to an edge. Press the square's handle against the reference edge. Keeping the blade flat on the surface, draw a pencil along the outer edge *(above)*.

CARPENTER'S SQUARE

Gauge

Marking a line at 90° to an edge. Tip the square's long arm slightly downward and press it against the reference edge. Position the tip of a pencil and move the short arm to it, then draw the line *(above)*.

Marking a line at 45° to an edge. Screw gauges to the outer edges of the square's arms at the same distance from the corner. Butt the gauges against the reference edge and hold the square flat on the surface, then draw a pencil along the appropriate arm *(above)*.

COMBINATION SQUARE

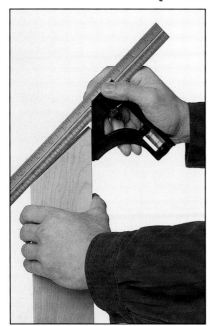

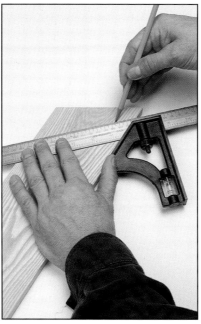

Checking for a 45° or 90° angle. Butt the 45° face of the square's handle against the reference surface to check for a 45° angle *(above)*. Check for a 90° angle the same way using the 90° face of the handle.

Marking 45° or 90° to an edge. Hold the 45° face of the square's handle against the reference edge to draw a line at a 45° angle *(above)*, the 90° face to draw a perpendicular line.

Marking parallel to an edge. Press the 90° face of the square's handle against the reference edge. Holding a pencil at the end of the blade, guide the handle smoothly along the reference edge *(above)*.

T-BEVEL

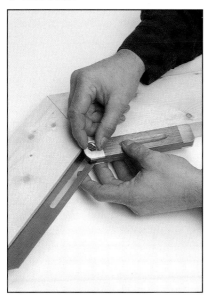

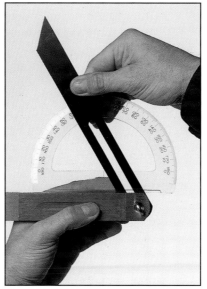

Copying an angle. Hold the bevel's handle against the reference edge and loosen the wing nut to slide the blade against the other edge. Set the angle by tightening the wing nut *(above)*.

Reading or setting an angle. Hold the bevel's handle at the base of a protractor, the blade's inner edge aligned at its center point. Read or set an angle using the point on the scale intersected by the blade's inner edge *(above)*.

Transferring an angle. Press the inner edge of the bevel's handle against the reference edge. Keeping the blade flat on the surface, draw along its outer edge *(above)*.

STRAIGHTEDGE

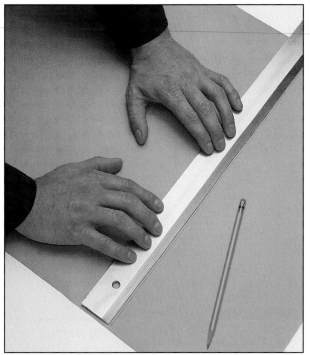

Inspecting a straightedge. Mark a line with one edge, then turn the straightedge around and align the same edge on the opposite side of the line *(above)*. If the edge deviates from the line, the straightedge is unsuitable for use.

Checking for flatness. Place the straightedge edge down *(above)* or flat across the surface at several locations and at different angles. A visible gap, as shown here, indicates that the surface is bowed.

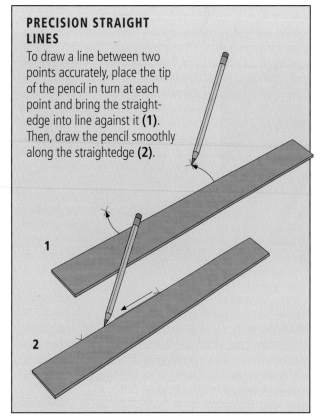

PRECISION STRAIGHT LINES

To draw a line between two points accurately, place the tip of the pencil in turn at each point and bring the straight-edge into line against it **(1)**. Then, draw the pencil smoothly along the straightedge **(2)**.

Marking a straight line. Lay the straightedge down flat, its beveled edge aligned with any marked end point. Hold the pencil against the beveled edge and draw along it *(above)*. Mark the same way using a utility knife or an awl.

Hammers

Curved-claw hammer
The most durable type has a head made of drop-forged steel weighing 16 ounces. The inside edges of the claw should be sharp enough to grip smooth nail shanks. The handle material you choose is mostly a matter of personal preference; a wood handle naturally absorbs shocks, but the type made of fiberglass or steel has a rubber sheathing that softens the grip. A fiberglass or steel handle will stay fixed in the head longer than wood.

Rubber mallet
The head weighs about a pound. A simple rubber mallet will serve most purposes, but for specific projects, choose a mallet with replaceable, screw-on faces—one of rubber for shaping sheet metal and tapping wooden joints together and one of plastic for driving wood chisels.

Ball-peen hammer
The head weighs about 16 ounces, and the poll— the striking part—is beveled and hardened to resist chipping.

Framing hammer
Best for large framing projects, this hammer has a 17-inch handle and a 24-ounce head.

Maul
A short-handled sledge-hammer or maul with a 2- or 4-pound head is more practical for most uses than a heavy, long-handled one.

Tack hammer
The head weighs 5 ounces and has a magnetized poll for holding tacks while you start them in the workpiece.

SAFETY FIRST

To protect your eyes, always put on a pair of goggles before hammering nails; chiseling masonry, mortar, or stone; driving stakes; or demolishing walls.

Fastening with Screws

Wood screw

Fastens wood or other material to wood. Head types include: flat for countersinking and concealing; round for easy removal; and oval for countersinking and appearance. Lengths of $\frac{1}{2}$ inch to 6 inches most typical; diameters range from 0 gauge (.06 inch) to 24 gauge (.372 inch).

Drywall screw

Bugle-shaped, flat-head screw fastens drywall to wood or metal. Three ranges common: 6 gauge from 1 inch to $2\frac{1}{4}$ inches; 8 gauge of $2\frac{1}{2}$ or 3 inches; 10 gauge of $3\frac{3}{4}$ inches.

Exterior screw

Self-starting, counter-sinking screw with protective coating for use in pressure-treated wood. Sizes from $1\frac{5}{8}$-inch 6 gauge to 6-inch 10 gauge available.

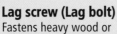

Lag screw (Lag bolt)

Fastens heavy wood or metal to wood (with washer under head) or to masonry (with shield of matching diameter). Hex or square head tightened using wrench. Available in lengths from 1 inch to 12 inches; diameters of $\frac{1}{4}$ and $\frac{3}{4}$ inch most common.

Plastic toggle

Used with wood screw for fastening medium-weight material to hollow wall. Sized to match diameter (gauge) of screw.

Lead or alloy anchor (shield)

Used with wood or lag screw for fastening heavy material to masonry. Sized to match diameter (gauge or inch) of fastener.

Plastic anchor

Used with wood screw for fastening light material to masonry or hollow wall. Sized to match four diameters (gauges) of screws: Nos. 4 to 6; Nos. 7 and 8; Nos. 10 and 12; and Nos. 14 to 16.

Masonry screw

Deep-threaded screw fastens light material to masonry. Head types include: flat for counter-sinking and concealing; and hex-washer for easy removal. Sizes from $1\frac{1}{4}$ to 4 inches in 12-gauge ($\frac{3}{16}$-inch) and 14-gauge ($\frac{1}{4}$-inch) diameters most common.

Sheet metal screw (Type F)

Chip-cutting screw fastens to metal or plastic from .05 to $\frac{1}{2}$ inch thick. Head types include pan, round, flat and hex. Typically available in No. 4 to No. 10 as well as $\frac{1}{4}$-, $\frac{5}{16}$- and $\frac{3}{8}$-inch diameters from $\frac{3}{16}$ inch to 3 inches in length.

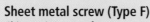

Sheet metal screw (Type A)

Gimlet-point screw fastens sheet metal to sheet metal or wood; also plywood or composition board to wood. Head types include pan, round and flat. Typically available in No. 2 to No. 14 as well as $\frac{5}{16}$- and $\frac{3}{8}$-inch diameters from $\frac{1}{4}$ inch to 3 inches in length.

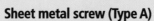

SCREWDRIVERS

Standard screwdriver
Typically plastic or wood handle molded onto regular, stubby or long shank. Available in different tip styles to match recesses of screw heads.

Offset screwdriver
Provides turning force in restricted spaces. Available in various sizes with same or different tip styles.

TIP STYLES

Flat

Cabinet

Phillips

Robertson

Torx

Hex

Ratchet screwdriver
Ratchet mechanism permits fast-action turning force. Interchangeable bits of different tip styles store in handle.

ELECTRIC DRILL ATTACHMENTS

Screwdriver bits
Available in different tip styles with or without holding collar.

Socket

Adjustable clutch driver
Sets interchangeable bits at different depths.

Drywall clutch driver
Fixed bit at preset depth for driving drywall screws.

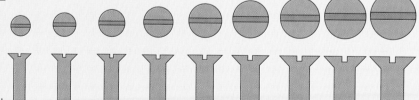

SCREW GAUGES

Screws of common diameters—gauge numbers—are represented life size. Information on the diameters of bits for pilot and clearance holes applies to screws regardless of their head shape, tip style or thread design.

Screw gauge	No. 4	No. 5	No. 6	No. 7	No. 8	No. 9	No. 10	No. 12	No. 14
Pilot hole	$\frac{1}{16}$"	$\frac{5}{64}$"	$\frac{5}{64}$"	$\frac{3}{32}$"	$\frac{3}{32}$"	$\frac{7}{64}$"	$\frac{7}{64}$"	$\frac{1}{8}$"	$\frac{9}{64}$"
Clearance hole	$\frac{1}{8}$"	$\frac{1}{8}$"	$\frac{9}{64}$"	$\frac{5}{32}$"	$\frac{11}{64}$"	$\frac{3}{16}$"	$\frac{13}{64}$"	$\frac{15}{64}$"	$\frac{1}{4}$"

INTO WOOD

HOLES FOR SCREWS

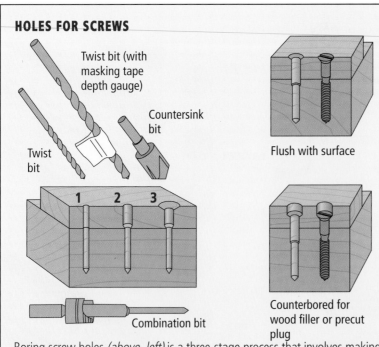

Boring screw holes *(above, left)* is a three-stage process that involves making: **1** a pilot hole equal to about $\frac{1}{3}$ the screw length; **2** a clearance hole the diameter of the screw shank through the piece being fastened; and **3** a countersink hole for the screw head. Three bits may be used; or, all holes can be made at once with a combination bit. Screw heads can be set two ways *(above, right)*.

Fastening wood pieces. Bore pilot, clearance and countersink holes, then assemble the pieces and drive in the screws *(above)*. Set the heads flush—as in the case here—or below the surface for concealing with filler or plugs.

EXTRACTOR FOR DAMAGED SCREWS

Drill a hole about $\frac{3}{8}$ inch deep into the center of the screw *(above, left)* using a twist bit of a size recommended for the extractor. Insert the extractor in the hole and turn it counterclockwise with a wrench *(above, right)* until it grips and backs out the screw.

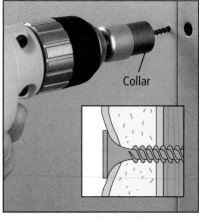

Screwing drywall to studs. Fit an electric drill with a drywall clutch driver. Seat the head of a drywall screw on the driver's bit, then press the tip into the drywall and start the drill *(above)*. Stop when the collar of the drywall touches the drywall and the head of the screw dimples the surface *(inset)*.

INTO MASONRY

  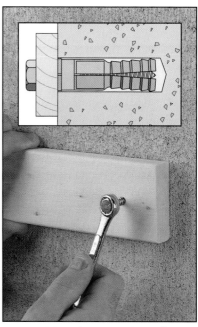

1 **Mark anchor (shield) locations** through clearance holes for lag screws bored in the piece being fastened *(above)*.

2 **Drill holes** for the anchors $\frac{1}{2}$ inch deeper than their length. Insert the anchors *(above)* and seat them flush with the surface.

3 **Position the piece** being fastened and drive in the lag screws with a wrench *(above)*, expanding the anchors so that they grip *(inset)*.

INTO HOLLOW MATERIAL

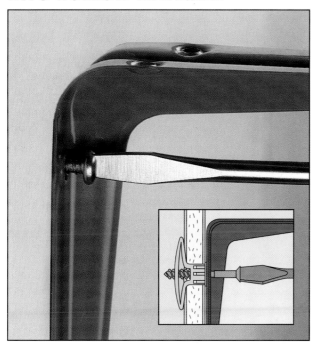 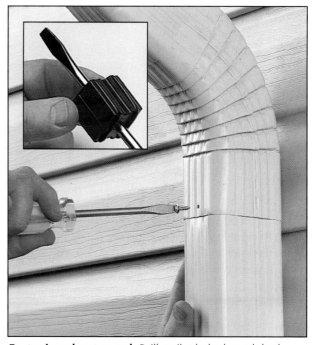

Mounting to drywall. Drill holes for toggles through the drywall. Insert the toggles, then position the item that is being mounted—in this case, a metal shelf support. Drive a screw into each toggle *(above)*, drawing it tightly against the drywall *(inset)*.

Fastening sheet metal. Drill a pilot hole through both pieces and a clearance hole through the piece being fastened. Magnetize a screwdriver *(inset)* so that it will hold the screw, then screw the pieces together *(above)*.

Cutters

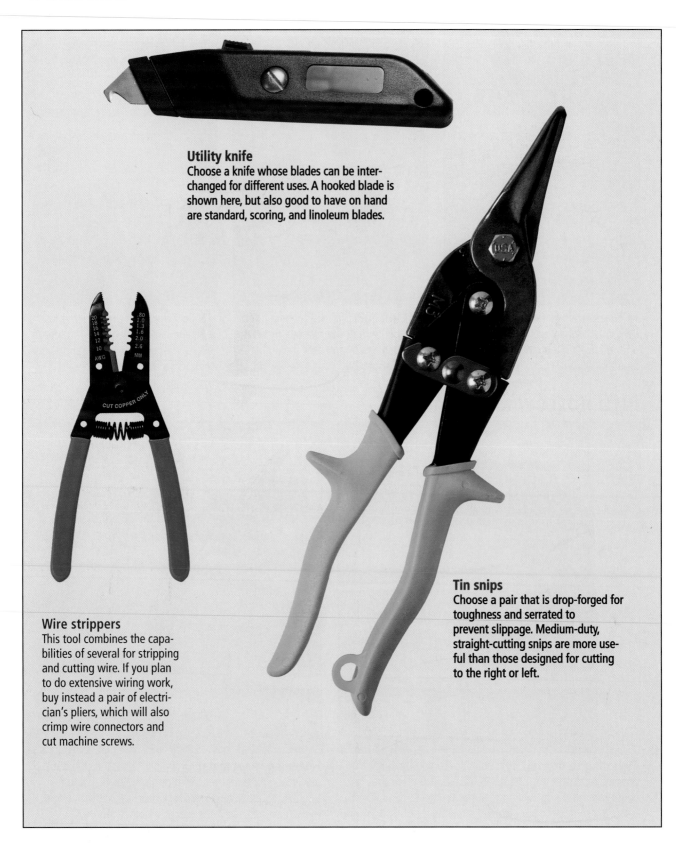

Utility knife
Choose a knife whose blades can be inter-changed for different uses. A hooked blade is shown here, but also good to have on hand are standard, scoring, and linoleum blades.

Wire strippers
This tool combines the capa-bilities of several for stripping and cutting wire. If you plan to do extensive wiring work, buy instead a pair of electri-cian's pliers, which will also crimp wire connectors and cut machine screws.

Tin snips
Choose a pair that is drop-forged for toughness and serrated to prevent slippage. Medium-duty, straight-cutting snips are more use-ful than those designed for cutting to the right or left.

Handsaws

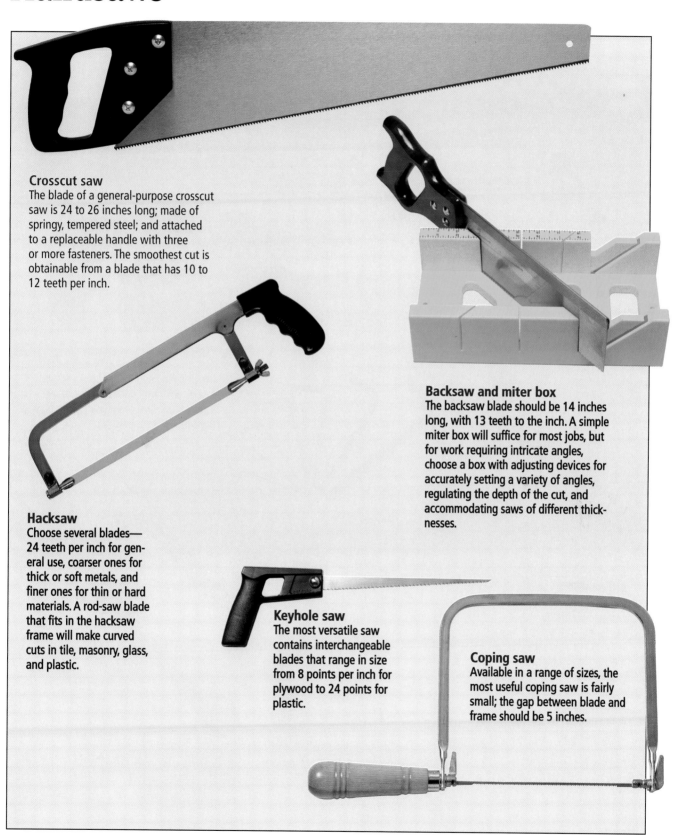

Crosscut saw
The blade of a general-purpose crosscut saw is 24 to 26 inches long; made of springy, tempered steel; and attached to a replaceable handle with three or more fasteners. The smoothest cut is obtainable from a blade that has 10 to 12 teeth per inch.

Backsaw and miter box
The backsaw blade should be 14 inches long, with 13 teeth to the inch. A simple miter box will suffice for most jobs, but for work requiring intricate angles, choose a box with adjusting devices for accurately setting a variety of angles, regulating the depth of the cut, and accommodating saws of different thicknesses.

Hacksaw
Choose several blades—24 teeth per inch for general use, coarser ones for thick or soft metals, and finer ones for thin or hard materials. A rod-saw blade that fits in the hacksaw frame will make curved cuts in tile, masonry, glass, and plastic.

Keyhole saw
The most versatile saw contains interchangeable blades that range in size from 8 points per inch for plywood to 24 points for plastic.

Coping saw
Available in a range of sizes, the most useful coping saw is fairly small; the gap between blade and frame should be 5 inches.

Wrenches

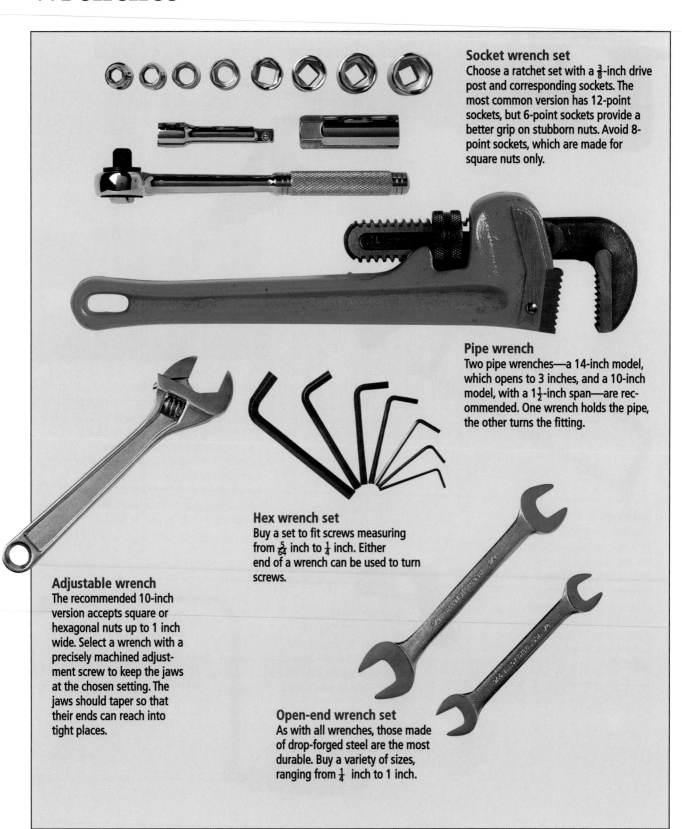

Socket wrench set
Choose a ratchet set with a $\frac{3}{8}$-inch drive post and corresponding sockets. The most common version has 12-point sockets, but 6-point sockets provide a better grip on stubborn nuts. Avoid 8-point sockets, which are made for square nuts only.

Pipe wrench
Two pipe wrenches—a 14-inch model, which opens to 3 inches, and a 10-inch model, with a $1\frac{1}{2}$-inch span—are recommended. One wrench holds the pipe, the other turns the fitting.

Hex wrench set
Buy a set to fit screws measuring from $\frac{5}{64}$ inch to $\frac{1}{4}$ inch. Either end of a wrench can be used to turn screws.

Adjustable wrench
The recommended 10-inch version accepts square or hexagonal nuts up to 1 inch wide. Select a wrench with a precisely machined adjustment screw to keep the jaws at the chosen setting. The jaws should taper so that their ends can reach into tight places.

Open-end wrench set
As with all wrenches, those made of drop-forged steel are the most durable. Buy a variety of sizes, ranging from $\frac{1}{4}$ inch to 1 inch.

Pliers and Clamps

Long-nose pliers
The recommended size
for home use is
7 inches, with a wire
cutter near the pivot
and plastic grips for
comfort.

Locking-grip pliers
A 10-inch model with curved jaws
can hold round objects almost 2 inches
thick; a wire cutter near the pivot will
come in handy.

Slip-joint pliers
Choose an 8-inch pair whose
drop-forged jaws have sharp ser-
rations to hold work tightly; it
should have a wire cutter near
the pivot and scored
handles for a secure grip.

Channel-joint pliers
Choose a 12-inch model
with long handles—
often plastic coated for
comfort—that allow a
tight grip on objects up
to 2 inches thick.

C-clamp
The head on top of the screw
should swivel freely so that the
clamp will grip surfaces that
are not quite parallel. The
swivel feature also prevents
the clamp from "walking" as it
is tightened.

Spring clamp
Also handy for quick
clamping jobs, these
are available in sizes
up to 8 inches long,
with jaws that open 3
inches or more.
Handles and tips are
sheathed in resilient
plastic.

Quick clamp
As the name implies, this clamp is easier
to tighten than a C-clamp. Some have an
attachment that holds right-angle joints.

Planes and Files

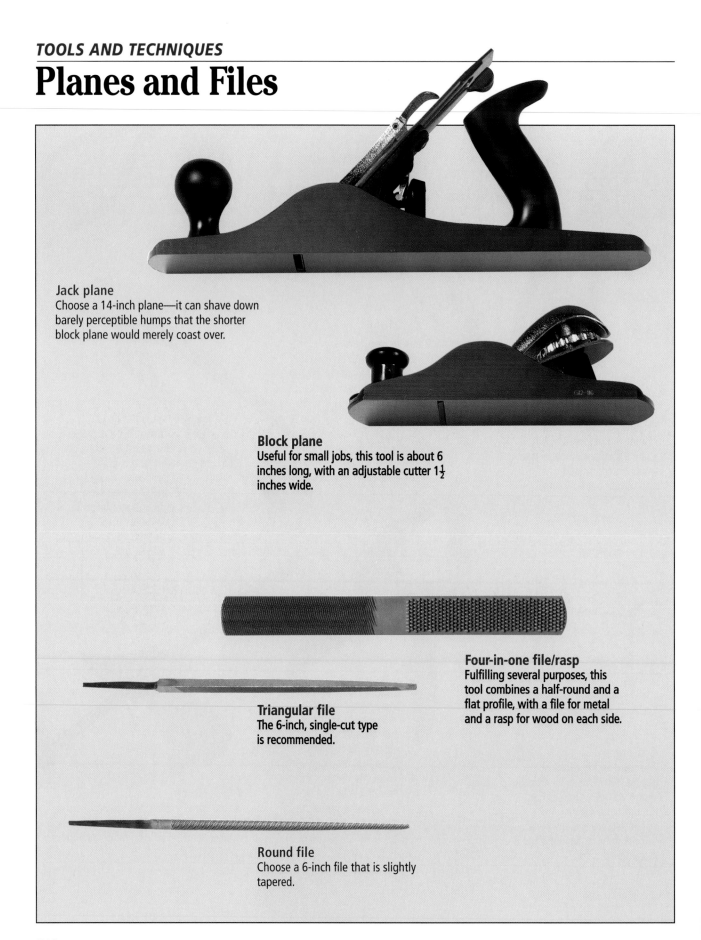

Jack plane
Choose a 14-inch plane—it can shave down barely perceptible humps that the shorter block plane would merely coast over.

Block plane
Useful for small jobs, this tool is about 6 inches long, with an adjustable cutter $1\frac{1}{2}$ inches wide.

Four-in-one file/rasp
Fulfilling several purposes, this tool combines a half-round and a flat profile, with a file for metal and a rasp for wood on each side.

Triangular file
The 6-inch, single-cut type is recommended.

Round file
Choose a 6-inch file that is slightly tapered.

Chisels, Awls, & Punches

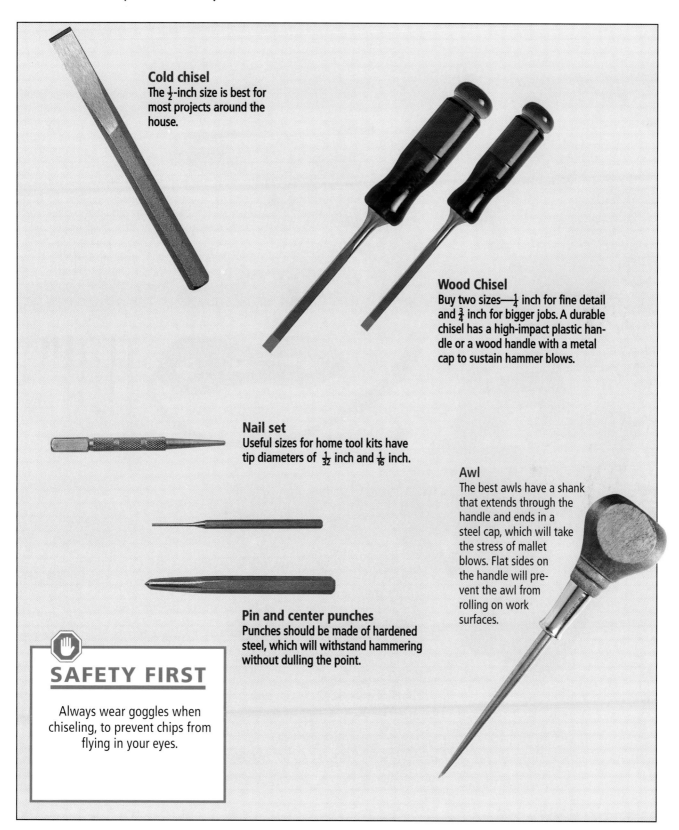

Cold chisel
The $\frac{1}{2}$-inch size is best for most projects around the house.

Wood Chisel
Buy two sizes—$\frac{1}{4}$ inch for fine detail and $\frac{3}{4}$ inch for bigger jobs. A durable chisel has a high-impact plastic handle or a wood handle with a metal cap to sustain hammer blows.

Nail set
Useful sizes for home tool kits have tip diameters of $\frac{1}{32}$ inch and $\frac{1}{16}$ inch.

Awl
The best awls have a shank that extends through the handle and ends in a steel cap, which will take the stress of mallet blows. Flat sides on the handle will prevent the awl from rolling on work surfaces.

Pin and center punches
Punches should be made of hardened steel, which will withstand hammering without dulling the point.

SAFETY FIRST

Always wear goggles when chiseling, to prevent chips from flying in your eyes.

Power Tools

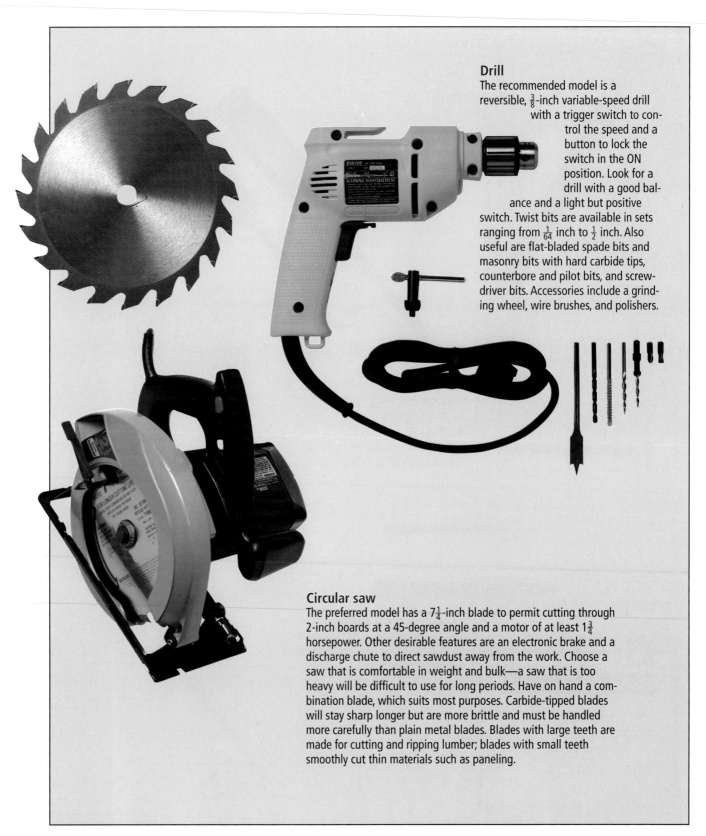

Drill

The recommended model is a reversible, $\frac{3}{8}$-inch variable-speed drill with a trigger switch to control the speed and a button to lock the switch in the ON position. Look for a drill with a good balance and a light but positive switch. Twist bits are available in sets ranging from $\frac{1}{64}$ inch to $\frac{1}{2}$ inch. Also useful are flat-bladed spade bits and masonry bits with hard carbide tips, counterbore and pilot bits, and screwdriver bits. Accessories include a grinding wheel, wire brushes, and polishers.

Circular saw

The preferred model has a $7\frac{1}{4}$-inch blade to permit cutting through 2-inch boards at a 45-degree angle and a motor of at least $1\frac{3}{4}$ horsepower. Other desirable features are an electronic brake and a discharge chute to direct sawdust away from the work. Choose a saw that is comfortable in weight and bulk—a saw that is too heavy will be difficult to use for long periods. Have on hand a combination blade, which suits most purposes. Carbide-tipped blades will stay sharp longer but are more brittle and must be handled more carefully than plain metal blades. Blades with large teeth are made for cutting and ripping lumber; blades with small teeth smoothly cut thin materials such as paneling.

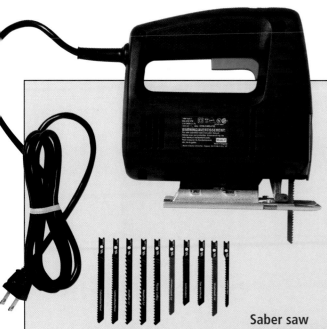

Saber saw

For a home workshop, buy a variable-speed saber saw that has at least $\frac{1}{2}$ horsepower. Choose a saw that cuts bevels and that blows sawdust from the cutting line. For this sized saw, buy blades 4 inches long or less, to avoid overtaxing the motor. The more teeth per inch, the smoother the cut. Keep on hand an assortment of blades for cutting wood, metal, plastic, and ceramic tile; add others as needed for cutting fiberglass or plaster.

Router

For home use, buy a router with at least a $\frac{3}{4}$-horsepower motor. A saw that accepts a $\frac{1}{4}$-inch bit shank is suitable for most purposes, but for detailed routing jobs, those that accept a $\frac{1}{2}$-inch shank have the best selection of bits. Safety and convenience features include a plastic chip deflector, a quick-stop switch, and a depth scale on the housing. Two simple bits do most home routing jobs—a straight bit and a rabbet bit. For detailed woodworking, there is a wide range of bits for specific jobs.

Orbital sander

For average sanding jobs, a palm orbital sander is small and easy to handle. Choose a direct-drive model—with the motor connected directly to the pad and a pad that makes a $\frac{1}{8}$-inch or smaller orbit at the rate of at least 9,000 orbits per minute. A dust collector is a handy additional feature; for sanding lead-containing paint (see page 219) choose a sander that can be equipped with an HEPA filter.

SAFETY FIRST

Safety is as important as skill in the operation of power tools, and a few rules apply in every situation: If you are working with old material, follow the precautions on pages 219-20 in case it contains lead or asbestos. Dress for the job. Avoid loose clothing, tuck in your shirt, and roll up your sleeves. Tie back long hair. Do not wear gloves when using power tools, for they reduce dexterity and can catch in moving parts. To keep wood dust and shavings out of your eyes, always wear goggles. In an enclosed space, earplugs or noise mufflers reduce the racket to a safe level. Don a dust mask when working with pressure-treated lumber. Always wear goggles when chiseling, to prevent chips from flying in your eyes.

Plumber's Aids

Plumber's auger
The recommended type resembles a tightly wound steel spring 10 feet long, with a crank handle.

Closet auger
Similar to a trap-and-drain auger, this tool is designed for unclogging toilets.

Plunger
The most practical style has a collapsible flange that adapts to several types of drains.

General Tools

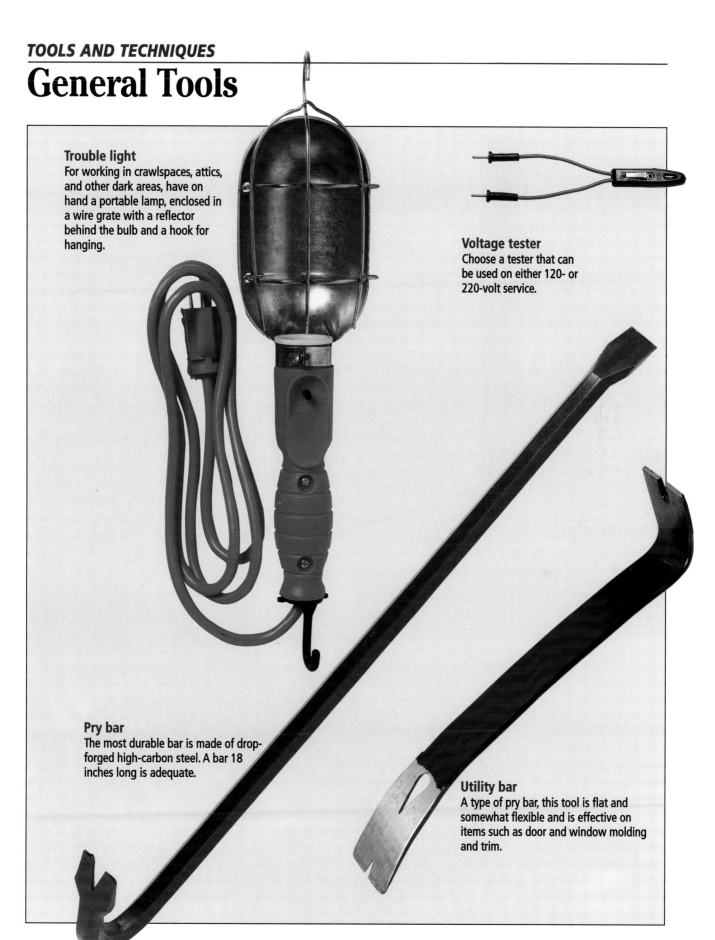

Trouble light
For working in crawlspaces, attics, and other dark areas, have on hand a portable lamp, enclosed in a wire grate with a reflector behind the bulb and a hook for hanging.

Voltage tester
Choose a tester that can be used on either 120- or 220-volt service.

Pry bar
The most durable bar is made of drop-forged high-carbon steel. A bar 18 inches long is adequate.

Utility bar
A type of pry bar, this tool is flat and somewhat flexible and is effective on items such as door and window molding and trim.

General Tools

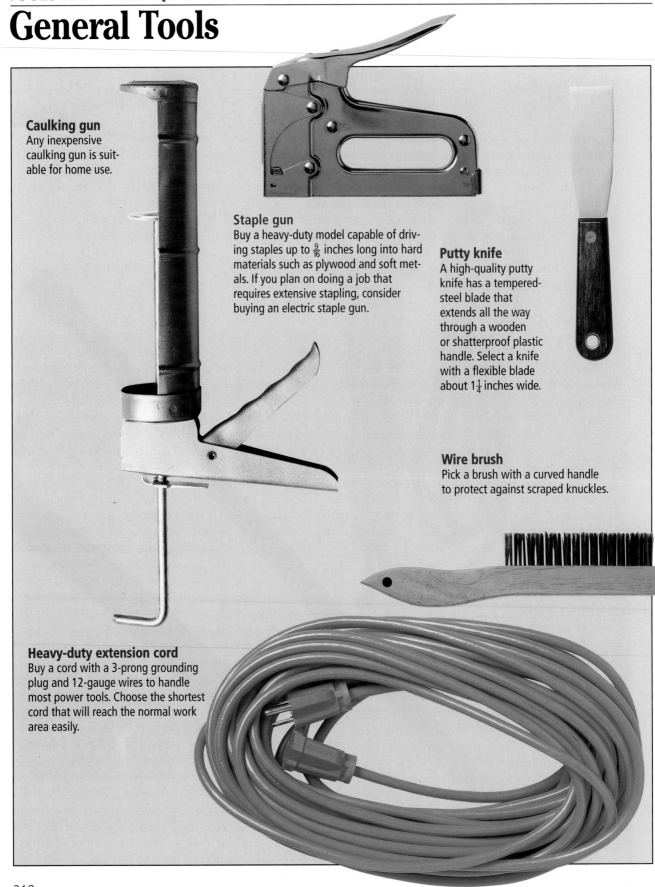

Caulking gun
Any inexpensive caulking gun is suitable for home use.

Staple gun
Buy a heavy-duty model capable of driving staples up to $\frac{9}{16}$ inches long into hard materials such as plywood and soft metals. If you plan on doing a job that requires extensive stapling, consider buying an electric staple gun.

Putty knife
A high-quality putty knife has a tempered-steel blade that extends all the way through a wooden or shatterproof plastic handle. Select a knife with a flexible blade about $1\frac{1}{4}$ inches wide.

Wire brush
Pick a brush with a curved handle to protect against scraped knuckles.

Heavy-duty extension cord
Buy a cord with a 3-prong grounding plug and 12-gauge wires to handle most power tools. Choose the shortest cord that will reach the normal work area easily.

Dealing with Hazards

Disposal of paints

The chemicals in paint are environmentally hazardous. You can help your town reduce the cost of disposing of old paint as hazardous waste in the following ways.

Use up leftovers as a prime coat or offer them to others: neighbors, group homes, theatre groups, for example.
Also try calling your local sanitation office to find out what days it may be able to pick up paints for recycling.

Evaporate the liquid from latex paint and small quantities of oil-based paint by taking the lid off and leaving it outdoors where flames, children and pets cannot get to it. The remaining solids are non-hazardous, household trash.

If you have more than 2 inches left in a can, absorb it by pouring clay-based kitty litter into the can and stirring until the liquid is absorbed, then replace the lid. A faster method is to pour the paint into a box of kitty litter, stirring as you add it. After closing the box or can, it may be discarded as household trash.

For purposes of designating a paint can as non-hazardous household trash most states specify less than 1 inch of residue in the bottom. If there is no remaining paint residue in a paint or aerosol can, it can be included in your town's scrap metal recycling area.

Lead and asbestos

Lead and asbestos, known health hazards, pervade houses constructed, remodeled, or redecorated before 1978. When disturbed, as they are likely to be during remodeling jobs, they pose a threat unless handled carefully. By observing the precautions listed below, you can safely deal with lead- or asbestos-laden building materials. Or consider hiring a contractor licensed in hazardous-substance removal or abatement—especially for a large project indoors. A professional is advisable if you suffer from cardiac or respiratory problems or don't tolerate heat well; the work requires a tightly fitted respirator and protective clothing that's hot to wear. Tackle a roof only if you are experienced in working at heights, keeping in mind that a respirator impairs vision.

Lead is found primarily in paint. Home test kits for lead in paint are available at hardware stores, or call your local health department or environmental protection office for other testing options.

Asbestos was once a component of wallboard, joint compound, insulation, flooring, and associated adhesives, as well as roofing felt, shingles and flashing.
When removing small samples of such materials for testing, mist the area with a mixture of 1 teaspoon low-sudsing detergent for each quart of water to suppress dust. Then take the samples to a local lab certified by the National Institute of Standards and Technology.

To remove materials containing lead or asbestos:

• Keep people and pets away from the area.
• Wear protective clothing (available from a safety-equipment supply house or paint stores) and wear a dual-cartridge respirator that has an HEPA filter.
• Indoors, seal off openings to the work area from the rest of the house with 6-mil polyethylene sheeting and duct tape. Cover rugs and furniture that can't be removed from the work area with more sheeting and tape. Turn off air conditioning and forced-air heating systems and seal the registers with plastic.
• Outdoors, cover the ground in the work area with 6-mil polyethylene sheeting. Never work in windy conditions. To remove shingles on a roof or exterior wall, pry up shingles, starting at the top, misting as you go. Place all debris in a polyethylene bag; never throw roofing or siding containing asbestos to the ground.
• Never sand asbestos-laden materials or cut them with power machinery. Instead, mist them with water and detergent, and remove them carefully with a hand tool. Likewise, use a hand tool for cutting materials covered with lead paint. If you must sand lead-painted materials with a power tool, do so with a sander equipped with an HEPA filter vacuum.
• When you finish indoor work, mist the plastic sheeting and roll it up, dusty side in. On bare floors, mop the area twice; on carpets, run a vacuum cleaner equipped with an HEPA filter.

continued on next page

Dealing with Hazards

• Take off protective clothing—including shoes—before leaving the work area. Wash the clothing separately from your other laundry. Shower and wash your hair immediately.

• Dispose of the materials as recommended by your local health department or environmental protection office.

Pressure-treated lumber

Arsenic compounds are used as a preservative on pressure-treated lumber. When handling this material, put on a pair of work gloves or wash your hands thoroughly after the job is done; while using power tools such as saws and sanders, wear a dust mask or respirator.

Chemicals

Many remodeling projects and repairs require products that contain toxic chemicals. Examples are paint and paint strippers, solvents, and related finishes; heavy-duty cleaning agents such as those intended for masonry, tile, and porcelain; drain uncloggers; mortars; sealants; and adhesives. Always read the cautions on the label before buying or using any of these products, and follow the manufacturer's directions for use. Wear a pair of nonporous gloves during the job, and work in a well-ventilated room or wear a respirator recommended for use with the specific product.

Shutting off the electricity

If the area around the service panel is flooded, call your local electricity utility company to shut off the power. If the area around the service panel is wet or damp, stand on a dry board or wear rubber boots. Wear heavy rubber gloves and use only one hand; keep the other hand behind your back, away from anything metal. At a circuit breaker panel, flip the circuit breaker for the circuit to OFF. If the circuit is not labeled, flip the main circuit breaker to OFF; the main circuit breaker is a linked double breaker, usually above the others and labeled MAIN. At a fuse panel, grasp the plug fuse for the circuit by its insulated rim and unscrew it. If the circuit is not labeled, grip the main fuse block by its handle and pull it straight out; if there is more than one main fuse block, pull out each one the same way. If there is no main circuit breaker or main fuse block, locate the service disconnect breaker in a separate box nearby or outdoors by the electricity meter and flip it to OFF.

Heights

When using a stepladder, always be sure the legs are fully open with the side braces locked in position. Never climb higher than one step from the top. Never place the ladder on an unstable or uneven surface. Try to avoid setting up your ladder where it could be struck by a door.

If you have to climb onto the roof, choose a dry day with little wind, and wear rubber-soled shoes. Make sure your extension ladder reaches 2 to 3 feet above the eaves to give you something to hold onto as you climb between the ladder and the roof. Have someone hold the bottom of the ladder while you're climbing, and if possible tie the top of the ladder to something solid to keep it from slipping sideways.

Dealing with Emergencies

Freeing a victim from the source of electrical shock

A person who contacts live current is usually thrown back from the source; sometimes, however, muscles contract involuntarily around the source. Do not touch the victim or the source. Immediately shut off the power (see "Shutting off the electricity"). If the power cannot be shut off immediately, protect your hand with a thick, dry towel or heavy work glove and unplug the source. Or, use a wooden broom handle or other wooden implement to knock the victim free.

Handling a victim of electrical shock

Call for medical help immediately. Check the victim's breathing and pulse. If there is no breathing, administer artificial respiration; if there is no pulse, administer cardiopulmonary resuscitation (CPR) if you are qualified. If the victim is breathing and has no back or neck injury, place him or her in the recovery position, tilting the head back with the face to one side and the tongue forward to maintain an open airway. Keep the victim calm until medical help arrives.

Escaping toxic vapors

Leave the work area immediately; go outdoors for fresh air. Remove any clothing splashed by chemicals or other caustic substances; loosen clothing at the waist, chest and neck. If you feel faint, sit with your head lowered between your knees. Have someone ventilate the work area and close all containers. Call your local poison control center for medical help.

Flushing caustic substances from the skin

Gently remove any clothing from the injury—unless it has adhered to the skin. If the injury is severe, cover it with a gauze dressing and seek medical help immediately. Otherwise, flush the skin with a gentle flow of cold water for at least 5 minutes, then bandage it with a gauze dressing. Launder any affected clothing before rewearing it.

Flushing chemicals from eyes

Holding the eyelids of the injured eye apart, position the eye under a gentle flow of cool water from a faucet or pitcher; tilt the head to one side to prevent the chemical from washing into the uninjured eye. Flush the eye for 15 to 30 minutes, then cover both eyes with gauze dressings to prevent eye movement. Seek medical help immediately.

Shutting off the water supply

To turn off the main water supply, locate the main shutoff valve on the main water supply pipe for the house and close it. Usually it is found at the entry point of the main water supply pipe, indoors near the water meter or elsewhere in the basement, utility room or crawlspace. If your water supply is provided by a well, look for the main shutoff valve on the main water supply pipe near the pressure gauge or water pump. Turn the handle fully clockwise to close the valve, shutting off the water supply. If the water has two valves, close the valve on the supply side (before the water meter). To drain the water supply pipes in the house, open all the faucets.

CALENDAR OF HOME MAINTENANCE

*By performing routine home maintenance, you can extend the life span of
your house and prevent minor problems from becoming costly disasters.*

KEY	
▬	monthly
▬	seasonally (4 times a year)
▬	biannually
▬	annually

Heating & Cooling Systems

▬ Clean and check forced-air heating and cooling filters.

▬ Dust heating and cooling system thermostat and check to see that it is level.

▬ Clean and check the shut-off valves of convectors or radiators.

▬ Remove dust from the air conditioning unit or dehumidifier by vacuuming or brushing the evaporator coils.

▬ Clean or replace the filter of the central air conditioning unit. Trim shrubbery surrounding unit.

Appliances

▬ Clean grease from the inside of the kitchen range hood, and check the filter—either clean or replace it.

▬ Remove dust from the condenser of the refrigerator with a vacuum.

▬ Drain the sediment from the bottom of the water heater and boiler.

▬ Check cords or plugs of various electrical appliances around the house. If they are worn, repair or replace them.

Safety & Security

▬ Charge or replace smoke detector batteries.

▬ Check gauges on fire extinguishers to make sure they are fully charged.

Roof & Chimney

▬ Clean and inspect the gutters. Remove waste and secure any loose straps or hangers.

▬ Inspect the roof and repair damaged shingles or cracks in roll roofing. Check to make sure the flashing is secure and in good condition.

▬ Check soot buildup in the chimney and check to see that the damper is working.

Exterior, Foundation, & Grounds

▬ Repair damaged or decaying exterior siding, masonry, or stucco. Fill in cracks or recaulk.

▬ Inspect the exterior and foundation of your home for termites and carpenter ants.

▬ Check and replace worn weatherstripping.

▬ Exchange glass and screens in storm doors and windows.

▬ In the winter, shut off hose connections to avoid freezing

▬ Pour two buckets of water into the pit of the sump pump to test the motor and pump.

IMPORTANT TELEPHONE NUMBERS

Community Services   *name*   *phone*

Water Company   ....

Telephone Company   ....

Power Company   ....

Gas Company   ....

Trash/Recycling   ....

other   ....

other   ....

Repair Services   *name*   *phone*

Electrician   ....

Plumber   ....

Roofer   ....

Heating/AC Service   ....

Painter   ....

Carpenter   ....

Appliance Repair   ....

other   ....

other   ....

Hot Lines

U.S. Environmental Protection Agency   800-228-8711

Consumer Product Safety Commission Hot Line   800-638-2772

Pesticide Hot Line   800-858-7378